AN INTRODUCTION TO

The American Legal System

A SUPPLEMENT TO

Higher
Education
AND THE
Law

by

Harry T. Edwards
CIRCUIT JUDGE
UNITED STATES COURT OF APPEALS
FOR THE DISTRICT OF COLUMBIA CIRCUIT

and

Virginia Davis Nordin
ASSISTANT PROFESSOR OF EDUCATIONAL ADMINISTRATION
UNIVERSITY OF WISCONSIN - MADISON

INSTITUTE FOR EDUCATIONAL MANAGEMENT
HARVARD UNIVERSITY
CAMBRIDGE, MASSACHUSETTS

AN INTRODUCTION TO

The American Legal System

A SUPPLEMENT TO

Higher
Education
Law
AND THE

An Introduction to
THE AMERICAN LEGAL SYSTEM
A Supplement to
HIGHER EDUCATION AND THE LAW

Copyright © 1980 by:

HARRY T. EDWARDS
Circuit Judge
5818 United States Court of Appeals
Third and Constitution Avenues, N.W.
Washington, D.C.   20001

VIRGINIA DAVIS NORDIN
Assistant Professor of Educational Administration
University of Wisconsin
Madison, Wisconsin   53706

International Standard Book Number: 0-934222-02-9
Library of Congress Catalogue Card Number: 80-82033

Published by:
INSTITUTE FOR EDUCATIONAL MANAGEMENT
HARVARD UNIVERSITY
CAMBRIDGE, MASSACHUSETTS 02138

The authors wish to acknowledge, with sincere gratitude,
the assistance given to them by
Phoebe Salten, Esq.
Ms. Salten's exceptional research and writing
efforts proved to be invaluable in the preparation of this booklet.

PREFACE

This booklet has been designed to serve as a supplement to *Higher Education and the Law* (Institute for Educational Management, Harvard University, Cambridge, Massachusetts, 1979). The main purpose of this supplement is to give a brief description of the American legal system for scholars, students and administrators in the field of higher education who have had little or no legal training.

It is our hope that the materials included in this booklet will assist non-lawyers in understanding the legal process in the United States and, thus, facilitate their use of the more comprehensive materials found in the basic text.

No attempt has been made to write a fully definitive work on the American legal system. Such an effort would itself require another complete text. Rather, this supplement, with applicable references included, is merely an overview of the legal system presently in place in the United States.

Harry T. Edwards

Virginia Davis Nordin

June, 1980

TABLE OF CONTENTS

PAGE

CHAPTER 1—Introduction   1

CHAPTER 2—The United States Courts   3

CHAPTER 3—The Process of Judicial Review   11

CHAPTER 4—Reading and Understanding Judicial Opinions   19

CHAPTER 5—State Court Systems   23

CHAPTER 6—Legislative and Statutory Sources of Law   25

CHAPTER 7—Administrative Rules and Regulations
          As Sources of Law   39

APPENDIX A—Bibliography   43

APPENDIX B—The United States Constitution   47

CHAPTER 1

INTRODUCTION

The study of "higher education and the law" can no longer be regarded solely as a matter of academic interest for those in the higher education community. As the realities of the nineteen-eighties unfold, colleges and universities simply cannot afford to structure their responses to the American legal system in terms of the once privileged "ivory tower" status of academic institutions. For better or worse, the sixties and seventies have witnessed the demise of various legal doctrines which traditionally insulated certain officials and institutions from legal challenges to their official acts. The gradual erosion of the doctrines of governmental and charitable immunities serves as a prime example of this trend.

During this period of dramatic expansion in the regulation of American institutions generally—whether in the public or private sectors, whether industrial, medical, political or educational—academic institutions have increasingly come to be viewed as appropriate targets for legal control. For this reason one can no longer fully comprehend the workings of colleges and universities, either internally or as they relate to and interact with other forces in society, without some serious study of how "the law" affects the higher education community.

At one level of abstraction, college and university law concerns itself with constitutional and statutory structural issues: questions about the nature of an academic institution as a legal entity and about the basis for the power to create, govern and operate schools, both public and private. At the other extreme, the demands daily faced by a college administrator require concrete, particularized answers to questions that implicate most, if not all, of the traditional disciplines of substantive law. Issues in tort and contract law, equal opportunity, zoning, and environmental regulation might well underlie the routine decisions made by a college administrator in the course of a relatively uneventful week.

For the student of the university, the task of learning to operate within the context of American "law" is a challenging one. The legal systems of the United States, premised on federalism, involve a multiplicity of courts, laws and jurisdictions. While the United States Constitution, as interpreted by the Supreme Court of the United States, governs the most fundamental questions concerning the distribution of state and federal powers, that same Constitution creates a federal government of limited powers and federal courts of limited jurisdiction. Yet, the question of federal/state relations is hardly susceptible of simple analysis. For example, the Tenth Amendment to the United States Constitution explicitly provides that those powers not delegated to the federal government by the Constitution are "reserved to the states respectively, or to the people." However, the Commerce Clause, in Article I, Section 8 of the Constitution, has been construed broadly to allow

1

Congress to regulate a wide variety of activities in "interstate commerce" and the Fourteenth Amendment has also been construed broadly to guarantee "equal protection of the laws" for citizens of all states. As a consequence, federal/state relations cannot be adequately described by a static hierarchical structure. This area of the law and the relationships it defines are in a process of constant evolution.

The educator and educational administrator are part of an institution which must operate as a coherent entity in the context of the multiplicity, ambiguity and change which characterize the American legal system. That institution will be subject to the legal system and subsystems of one of the fifty states. It will operate within the federal sphere as well, subject to federal laws, federal administrative action and the jurisdiction of one or more federal courts. What follows is intended as a summary guide to the geography of this intricate and complex area. Clearly, a more detailed analysis or a fully accurate description of any of its features would require a lengthy volume and be a course of study in itself. It is hoped that once some landmarks have been identified and patterns explicated, the student can proceed on his intended journey through the areas of federal and state constitutional, statutory and administrative law with at least a general awareness of the legal system in the United States and the "laws" produced by that system.

CHAPTER 2

THE UNITED STATES COURTS

REPORT BY THE COMMITTEE ON THE JUDICIARY, UNITED STATES HOUSE OF REPRESENTATIVES (1975)

The position of the United States courts in our governmental organization is not difficult to understand when that organization is seen as a whole. Our government is a dual one—Federal and State—and the Federal Government in turn has three separate branches—the Legislative, the Executive, and the Judicial. The United States courts constitute the Judicial Branch of the Federal Government. Thus, the powers of the United States courts are first of all limited as Federal powers—they can exercise only those powers granted by the United States Constitution to the Federal Government —and secondly are limited as judicial—they cannot exercise powers belonging to the Legislative or Executive Branches of the Government.

THE JUDICIAL BRANCH

The Constitution assures the equality and independence of the Judicial Branch from the Legislative and Executive Branches. Although Federal judges are appointed by the President of the United States with the advice and consent of the Senate, and although funds for the operation of the courts are appropriated by the Congress, the independence of the United States courts is provided for in three respects:

First, under the Constitution these courts can be called upon to exercise only judicial powers and to perform only judicial work. Judicial power and judicial work involve essentially the application and interpretation of the law in the decision of real differences, that is, in the language of the Constitution, the decision of "Cases" and "Controversies." The courts cannot be called upon to make laws—the function of the Legislative Department—nor to enforce and execute laws—the function of the Executive Department.

Second, Federal judges "hold their Office during good Behavior," that is, as long as they desire to be judges and perform their work. They can be removed from office against their will only by impeachment.

Third, the Constitution provides that the "Compensation" of Federal judges "shall not be diminished during their continuance in office." Neither the President nor the Congress can reduce the salary of a Federal judge.

These three provisions—for judicial work only, for holding office during good behavior, and for undiminished compensation—are designed to assure judges of independence from outside influence so that their decisions may be completely impartial.

STATE AND UNITED STATES COURT SYSTEMS

Throughout the United States there are two sets of judicial systems. One set is that of the State and local courts established in each State under the authority of the State government. The other is that of the United States courts set up under the authority of the Constitution by the Congress of the United States.

The State courts have general, unlimited power to decide almost every type of case, subject only to the limitations of State law. They are located in every town and county and are the tribunals with which citizens most often have contact. The great bulk of legal business concerning divorce and the probate of estates and all other matters except those assigned to the United States courts is handled by these State courts.

The United States courts, on the other hand, have power to decide only those cases in which the Constitution gives them authority. They are located principally in the larger cities. The controversies in only a few carefully selected types of cases set forth in the Constitution can be heard in the United States courts.

CASES WHICH THE UNITED STATES COURTS CAN DECIDE

The controversies which can be decided in the United States courts are set forth in section 2 of Article III of the United States Constitution. These are first of all "Controversies to which the United States shall be a party," that is, cases in which the United States Government itself or one of its officers is either suing someone else or is being sued by another party. Obviously it would be inappropriate that the United States Government depend upon the State governments for the courts in which to decide controversies to which it is a party.

Secondly, the United States courts have power to decide cases where State courts are inappropriate or might be suspected of partiality. Thus, Federal judicial power extends "to Controversies between two or more States; between a State and Citizens of another State; between Citizens of different States; between Citizens of the same State claiming Lands under Grants of different States, * * *." If the State of Missouri sues the State of Illinois for pollution of the Mississippi River, the courts of either Missouri or Illinois would be inappropriate and perhaps not impartial forums. These suits may be decided in the United States courts. At various times State feeling in our country has run high, and it has seemed better to avoid any suspicion of favoritism by vesting power to decide these controversies in the United States courts.

State courts are also inappropriate in "Cases affecting Ambassadors, other public Ministers and Consuls" and in cases "between a State, or the Citizens thereof, and foreign States, Citizens, or Subjects." The United States Government has responsibility for our relations with other nations, and cases involving their representatives or their citizens may affect our foreign relations so that such cases should be decided in the United States courts.

And, thirdly the Constitution provides that the judicial power extends "to all Cases, in Law and Equity, arising under this Constitution, the Laws of the United States, and Treaties made, or which shall be made, under their Authority" and "to all Cases of admiralty and maritime jurisdiction." Under these provisions the United States courts decide cases involving the Constitution, laws enacted by Congress, treaties, or laws relating to navigable waters.

The Constitution declares what cases may be decided in the United States courts. The Congress can and has determined that some of these cases may also be tried in State courts and that others may be tried only in the United States courts. Thus Congress has provided that, with some exceptions, cases arising under the Constitution or laws of the United States or between citizens of different States may be tried in the United States courts only if the amount involved exceeds $10,000 and even then may be tried in either the State or the United States courts. The Congress has also provided that maritime cases and suits against consuls can be tried only in the United States courts. When a State court decides a case involving Federal law, it in a sense acts as a United States court, and its decision on Federal law may be reviewed by the United States Supreme Court.

In any event this discussion should make it clear that the United States courts cannot decide every case which arises, but only those which the Constitution and the laws enacted by the Congress allot to them. And as you may suspect from the length of this discussion, whether a case is one which may be decided by the United States courts is an extremely technical and complicated matter which lawyers and judges frequently spend a great deal of time resolving.

THE UNITED STATES COURT SYSTEM

The United States court system to which decision of the types of cases just discussed has been entrusted has varied a great deal throughout the history of our country. The Constitution merely provides: "The Judicial Power of the United States, shall be vested in one supreme Court, and in such inferior Courts as the Congress may from time to time ordain and establish." Thus, the only indispensable court is the Supreme Court, and the Congress has from time to time established and abolished various other United States courts.

At the present time the United States court system may be likened to a pyramid. At the apex of the pyramid stands the Supreme Court of the United States, the highest court in the land. On the next level stand the United States courts of appeals, 11 in all. On the next level stand the United States district courts, 94 in all, including the United States District Courts for the District of Columbia and Puerto Rico and the district courts in the Canal Zone, Guam, and the Virgin Islands. The United States Tax Court and, in a sense, certain administrative agencies may be included here because the review of their decisions may be directly in the courts of appeals. Some agency reviews, however, are handled by the district courts.

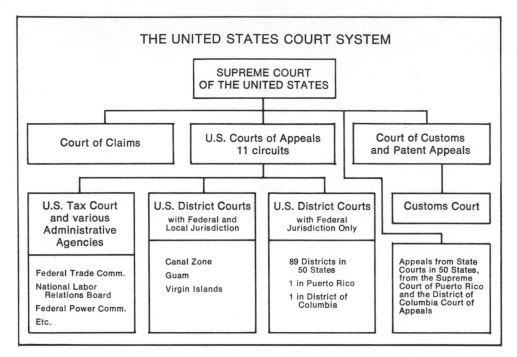

THE UNITED STATES COURT SYSTEM

SUPREME COURT
OF THE UNITED STATES

Court of Claims

U.S. Courts of Appeals
11 circuits

Court of Customs
and Patent Appeals

U.S. Tax Court
and various
Administrative
Agencies

U.S. District Courts
with Federal and
Local Jurisdiction

U.S. District Courts
with Federal
Jurisdiction Only

Customs Court

Federal Trade Comm.

National Labor
Relations Board

Federal Power Comm.

Etc.

Canal Zone

Guam

Virgin Islands

89 Districts in
50 States

1 in Puerto Rico

1 in District of
Columbia

Appeals from State
Courts in 50 States,
from the Supreme
Court of Puerto Rico
and the District of
Columbia Court of
Appeals

A person involved in a suit in a United States court may thus proceed through three levels of decision. His case will be heard and decided by one of the courts or agencies on the lower level. If either party is dissatisfied with the decision rendered, he may usually have review of right in one of the courts of appeals. Then, if he is still dissatisfied, but usually only if his case involves a matter of great national importance, he may obtain review in the Supreme Court of the United States.

This pyramidal organization of the courts serves two purposes. First, the Supreme Court and the courts of appeals can correct errors which have been made in the decisions in the trial courts. Secondly, these higher courts can assure uniformity of decision by reviewing cases where two or more lower courts have reached different results. The chart above shows the organization of the United States courts.

THE SUPREME COURT

The highest court is the Supreme Court of the United States. It consists of nine Justices, appointed for life by the President with the advice and consent of the United States Senate. One Justice is designated the Chief Justice. . . . The officers appointed by the Court include a Clerk to keep its records, a Marshal to maintain order and supervise the administrative affairs of the Court, a Reporter to publish its opinions, and a Librarian to serve the justices and the lawyers of the Supreme Court bar. Additionally the Chief Justice is authorized to appoint an Administrative Assistant.

The court meets on the first Monday of October each year. It continues in session usually until June and receives and disposes of about 5,000 cases each year. Most of these cases are disposed of by the brief decision that the subject matter is either not proper or not of sufficient importance to warrant full Court review. But each year between 200 and 250 cases of great importance and interest are decided on the merits. About half of these decisions are announced in full published opinions.

COURTS OF APPEALS

The intermediate appellate courts in the United States judicial system are the courts of appeals in 11 circuits. Each circuit includes three or more States, except the District of Columbia Circuit. . . . The States of Alaska and Hawaii and the territory of Guam are included in the ninth circuit, Puerto Rico is included in the first circuit, the Virgin Islands in the third circuit, and the Canal Zone in the fifth circuit. Each court consists of between 3 and 15 judges depending upon the amount of work in the circuit, and the judge with the longest service, who has not reached his 70th birthday, is the chief judge. . . .

. . . A disappointed suitor in a district court usually has a right to have the decision of his case reviewed by the court of appeals of his circuit. In addition to appeals from the district courts, the courts of appeals receive many cases to review actions of the tax court and various Federal administrative agencies for errors of law.

*   *   *

DISTRICT COURTS

The United States courts where cases are initially tried and decided are the district courts. There are 94 of these courts, 89 in the 50 States, and one each in the District of Columbia, the Canal Zone, Guam, Puerto Rico, and the Virgin Islands. Each State has at least one court; but many States have two or three districts, and California, Texas, and New York have four districts each. A district itself may be divided into divisions and may have several places where the court hears cases. Each district has from 1 to 27 judges depending upon the volume of cases which must be decided. For each district there is a clerk's office, a United States marshal's office, and one or more bankruptcy judges, United States magistrates, probation officers and court reporters. In addition, there is a United States attorney's office in each district. Further, each district court has a plan under which lawyers are provided for poor defendants in criminal cases. To assure adequate service full-time public defenders are appointed in those courts where criminal cases are numerous.

Some district courts, namely those in the Canal Zone, Guam, and the Virgin Islands, have jurisdiction over local cases as well as those arising under Federal law. These courts thus differ in several respects from the other 91 United States district courts. In these places the Federal Government does not share the judicial power as it does with the State governments in the several States, with the local government of the District of Columbia, and with the Commonwealth Government in Puerto Rico. Thus, these courts are not limited to the types of cases defined in the Constitution as part of the Federal judicial power, but decide all types of cases as do State courts. Then, too, the judges in the Canal Zone, Guam and the Virgin Islands are not appointed for life, but for terms of 8 years, and are not protected against diminution of their salaries during their terms of office. These courts may also be given duties which are not strictly judicial in nature.

Because of these differences, territorial courts have been called "legislative courts" to distinguish them from the "constitutional courts." The name indicates that these courts have been created, not in the exercise of Congress' power to establish courts under the judiciary article of the Constitution, but under its powers in the legislative article over the Territories and other fields of Federal authority.

*   *   *

LAW AND PROCEDURE IN THE UNITED STATES COURTS

The organization of the United States courts set up to handle the types of cases designated in the Constitution for decision by the Judicial Branch of the Federal Government has been described. For many years there was much confusion as to whether these types of cases were merely to be decided by a different court system or whether in addition they were to be decided according to different rules of law and a different procedure.

The question of the rule of law to apply in these types of cases was largely determined by the supremacy clause making the Constitution, statutes, and treaties of the United States Government the supreme law of the land. However, until 1938 the United States courts in suits between citizens of different States also purported to apply a general law, not the law of any State; but now it is settled that the law applied in the United States courts is the same as the law which would be applied in a State court in similar cases.

The question of procedure, conversely, was long governed by the rule that the United States courts, except where Federal statutes otherwise provided, followed the procedure of the courts in the State where they were sitting. However, again in 1938, Rules of Civil Procedure prepared by an advisory committee and approved by the Supreme Court became effective to give the United States courts their own rules of practice. And in 1946 Federal Rules of Criminal Procedure prepared in a similar fashion became effective. Both rules of practice have adopted the simplest, most modern, and best procedure and have been models for procedural reform in the States. In 1966 these Rules of Civil and Criminal Procedure were extensively revised and updated. Then in 1968 the Supreme Court adopted uniform Rules of Federal Appellate Procedure for the United States Courts of Appeals. The Supreme Court has also approved new Rules of Evidence governing the trial of civil and criminal cases in the United States district courts, and new comprehensive Rules of Procedure in Bankruptcy cases. Rules adopted by the Court must be approved by Congress before they become effective. Thus, today the United States courts decide cases involving citizens of different States according to the same rules of law as would govern the case in a State court, but decide them by Federal procedure.

ILLUSTRATION: AN AUTOMOBILE ACCIDENT

This whole rather complex problem of the various cases that may be tried in the United States courts may be illustrated for you by the story of an automobile collision. Bill Smith from Chicago, driving his car on an Illinois road, has a collision with another vehicle. Ordinarily no suit arising out of that accident could be tried in a United States court; it would be heard and decided in a State court. But if the other vehicle were an army truck driven by a soldier, Bill Smith may want to sue the United States, or the United States may decide to sue Bill Smith. In either event Bill Smith or the United States may commence a suit in the United States district court in Illinois.

If the other vehicle belonged to a private person who lived in Illinois, Bill Smith or the other owner may sue only in the State court, unless under certain circumstances the suit involved some provision of the Federal statutes or the Federal Constitution. If, on the other hand, the other vehicle belonged to John Jones who lived in St. Louis, Mo., then either John Jones or Bill Smith may sue in a United States district court because they were from different States.

These possible suits have been civil cases brought to compensate the parties for damage done, and it is unlikely that a criminal case brought by the Government would arise. Yet, if either Bill Smith or the other driver had been handling his car so recklessly as to warrant a criminal prosecution for reckless driving, manslaughter, etc., the suit would be brought by the State of Illinois in the State court. Let us suppose, however, that the other driver was in a car which he had stolen in Indiana and had driven into Illinois. Then that driver might be prosecuted by the United States Government in the United States district court under Federal law for transporting a stolen automobile from one State into another.

If either Bill Smith or his adversary is dissatisfied with the decision of the United States district court, he may appeal to a United States court of appeals, and if still dissatisfied after a decision by that court, he may seek review in the United States Supreme Court on questions of Federal law which arose in the proceedings. So you can see how an accident usually gives rise to suits which can be tried in State courts only, but which under special circumstances may be tried or reviewed in the United States courts.

* * *

CHAPTER 3

THE PROCESS OF
JUDICIAL REVIEW

That the framers of the United States Constitution created a system of government which embodies the principle of "separation of powers" is a fundamental tenet of American political life. Every school child is taught to view the independence and equality of the three branches of our federal government as essential safeguards of our democratic freedoms.

The Supremacy Clause of the United States Constitution declares the Constitution and laws and treaties made thereunder to be "the supreme Law of the Land." Article VI, clause 2. It is thus by our written Constitution that all three branches of government are bound. Since the early 1800s, it has been settled that the ultimate guardians and interpreters of that supreme law were to be federal judges. In *Marbury v. Madison,** the Supreme Court, in a seminal opinion by Chief Justice John Marshall, asserted its power to review the constitutional validity of actions taken by coordinate branches of the national government. The decision in *Marbury* states that:

> . . . The question, whether an act, repugnant to the constitution, can become the law of the land, is a question deeply interesting to the United States; but, happily, not of an intricacy proportioned to its interest. It seems only necessary to recognize certain principles, supposed to have been long and well established, to decide it.
>
> That the people have an original right to establish, for their future government, such principles, as in their opinion, shall most conduce to their own happiness is the basis on which the whole American fabric has been erected. The exercise of this original right is a very great exertion; nor can it, nor ought it, to be frequently repeated. The principles, therefore, so established, are deemed fundamental. And as the authority from which they proceed is supreme, and can seldom act, they are designed to be permanent.
>
> This original and supreme will organizes the government, and assigns to different departments their respective powers. It may either stop here, or establish certain limits not to be transcended by those departments.
>
> The government of the United States is of the latter description. The powers of the legislature are defined and limited; and that those limits may not be mistaken, or forgotten, the constitution is written. To what purpose are powers limited, and to what purpose is that limitation committed to writing, if these limits may, at

---

* 5 U.S. (1 Cranch) 137 (1803).

11

any time, be passed by those intended to be restrained? The distinction between a government with limited and unlimited powers is abolished, if those limits do not confine the persons on whom they are imposed, and if acts prohibited and acts allowed, are of equal obligation. It is a proposition too plain to be contested, that the constitution controls any legislative act repugnant to it; or, that the legislature may alter the constitution by an ordinary act.

Between these alternatives, there is no middle ground. The constitution is either a superior paramount law, unchangeable by ordinary means, or it is on a level with ordinary legislative acts, and, like other acts, is alterable when the legislature shall please to alter it.

If the former part of the alternative be true, then a legislative act, contrary to the constitution, is not law: if the latter part be true, then written constitutions are absurd attempts, on the part of the people, to limit a power in its own nature, illimitable.

Certainly all those who have framed written constitutions contemplate them as forming the fundamental and paramount law of the nation, and consequently, the theory of every such government must be, that an act of the legislature, repugnant to the constitution, is void.

This theory is essentially attached to a written constitution, and is consequently, to be considered, by this court, as one of the fundamental principles of our society. It is not therefore to be lost sight of in the further consideration of this subject.

If an act of the legislature, repugnant to the constitution, is void, does it, notwithstanding its invalidity, bind the courts, and oblige them to give it effect? Or, in other words, though it be not law, does it constitute a rule as operative as if it was a law? This would be to overthrow in fact what was established in theory; and would seem, at first view, an absurdity too gross to be insisted on. It shall, however, receive a more attentive consideration.

It is emphatically the province and duty of the judicial department to say what the law is. Those who apply the rule to particular cases must of necessity expound and interpret that rule. If two laws conflict with each other, the courts must decide on the operation of each.

So, if a law be in opposition to the constitution; if both the law and the constitution apply to a particular case, so that the court must either decide that case conformably to the law, disregarding the constitution; or conformably to the constitution, disregarding the law; the court must determine which of these conflicting rules govern the case. This is of the very essence of judicial duty. . . .

While it might seem anomalous that one of three "equal" branches should hold final authority to declare the law, the tension between the notion of coequal branches of government and the principle of judicial review was recognized and accepted by the principal architects of our constitutional structure. Alexander Hamilton in *The Federalist*,* justified the role of "the least dangerous branch" as follows:

> . . . Whoever attentively considers the different departments of power must perceive, that in a government in which they are separated from each other, the judiciary, from the nature of its functions, will always be the least dangerous to the political rights of the constitution; because it will be least in a capacity to annoy or injure them. The executive not only dispenses the honors, but holds the sword of the community. The legislature not only commands the purse, but prescribes the rules by which the duties and rights of every citizen are to be regulated. The judiciary on the contrary has no influence over either the sword or the purse, no direction either of the strength or of the wealth of the society, and can take no active resolution whatever. It may truly be said to have neither Force nor Will, but merely judgment; and must ultimately depend upon the aid of the executive arm even for the efficacy of its judgments.
>
> This simple view of the matter suggests several important consequences. It proves incontestably that the judiciary is beyond comparison the weakest of the three departments of power; that it can never attack with success either of the other two; and that all possible care is requisite to enable it to defend itself against their attacks. . . .
>
> The complete independence of the courts of justice is peculiarly essential in a limited constitution. By a limited constitution I understand one which contains certain specified exceptions to the legislative authority; such for instance as that it shall pass no bills of attainder, no ex post facto laws, and the like. Limitations of this kind can be preserved in practice no other way than through the medium of the courts of justice; whose duty it must be to declare all acts contrary to the manifest tenor of the constitution void. Without this, all the reservations of particular rights or privileges would amount to nothing.
>
> Some perplexity respecting the right of the courts to pronounce legislative acts void, because contrary to the constitution, has arisen from an imagination that the doctrine would imply a superiority of the judiciary to the legislative power. It is urged that the authority which can declare the acts of another void, must necessarily be superior to the one whose acts may be declared void. As this doctrine is of great importance in all the American constitutions, a brief discussion of the grounds on which it rests cannot be unacceptable.

---

* Hamilton, *The Federalist*, No. 78.

There is no position which depends on clearer principles, than that every act of a delegated authority, contrary to the tenor of the commission under which it is exercised, is void. No legislative act therefore contrary to the constitution can be valid. To deny this would be to affirm that the deputy is greater than his principal; that the servant is above his master; that the representatives of the people are superior to the people themselves; that men acting by virtue of powers may do not only what their powers do not authorise, but what they forbid.

If it be said that the legislative body are themselves the constitutional judges of their own powers, and that the construction they put upon them is conclusive upon the other departments, it may be answered, that this cannot be the natural presumption, where it is not to be collected from any particular provisions in the constitution. It is not otherwise to be supposed that the constitution could intend to enable the representatives of the people to substitute their *will* to that of their constituents. It is far more rational to suppose that the courts were designed to be an intermediate body between the people and the legislature, in order, among other things, to keep the latter within the limits assigned to their authority. The interpretation of the laws is the proper and peculiar province of the courts. A constitution is in fact, and must be, regarded by the judges as a fundamental law. It therefore belongs to them to ascertain its meaning as well as the meaning of any particular act proceeding from the legislative body. If there should happen to be an irreconcilable variance between the two, that which has the superior obligation and validity ought of course to be preferred; or in other words, the constitution ought to be preferred to the statute, the intention of the people to the intention of their agents.

Nor does this conclusion by any means suppose a superiority of the judicial to the legislative power. It only supposes that the power of the people is superior to both; and that where the will of the legislature declared in its statutes, stands in opposition to that of the people declared in the constitution, the judges ought to be governed by the latter, rather than the former. They ought to regulate their decisions by the fundamental laws, rather than by those which are not fundamental. . . .

[The] independence of the judges is equally requisite to guard the constitution and the rights of individuals from the effects of those ill humours which the arts of designing men, or the influence of particular conjunctures, sometimes disseminate among the people themselves, and which, though they speedily give place to better information and more deliberate reflection, have a tendency in the meantime to occasion dangerous innovations in the government, and serious oppressions of the minor party in the community. . . .

Thoughtful reflection on the structural implications of judicial review will clarify for the reader why the impact of "law" on a particular institution can often be analyzed most thoroughly and economically through the study of judicial opinions. For the educator or educational administrator, involvement with the courts in a litigation posture, while a realistic prospect, normally is not a significant part of the daily agenda. Judges neither "make" nor "enforce" the multiplicity of laws that impinge on the operation of an educational institution. Yet the courts, with power neither of "purse" nor of "sword," ultimately "say what the law is." This is why the student of "the law," even in areas affected by significant legislation or administrative rules, will be a student of judicial opinions and, necessarily, of the judicial system as well.

Because it is ultimately the task of the judiciary to "say what the law is," analysis of the bases for and methodology of such judicial declarations has been the focus of much scholarly and judicial thought. In an oft-cited passage from a famous series of lectures, Justice (then Judge) Benjamin Cardozo presents one view of the question:*

> . . . Our first inquiry should therefore be: Where does the judge find the law which he embodies in his judgment? There are times when the source is obvious. The rule that fits the case may be supplied by the constitution or by statute. If that is so, the judge looks no farther. The correspondence ascertained, his duty is to obey. The constitution overrides a statute, but a statute, if consistent with the constitution, overrides the law of judges. In this sense, judge-made law is secondary and subordinate to the law that is made by legislators. It is true that codes and statutes do not render the judge superfluous, nor his work perfunctory and mechanical. There are gaps to be filled. There are doubts and ambiguities to be cleared. There are hardships and wrongs to be mitigated if not avoided. Interpretation is often spoken of as if it were nothing but the search and the discovery of a meaning which, however obscure and latent, had nonetheless a real and ascertainable pre-existence in the legislator's mind. The process is, indeed, that at times, but it is often something more. The ascertainment of intention may be the least of a judge's troubles in ascribing meaning to a statute. . . . [T]he difficulties of so-called interpretation arise when the legislature has had no meaning at all; when the question which is raised on the statute never occurred to it; when what the judges have to do is, not to determine what the legislature did mean on a point which was present to its mind, but to guess

---

* Cardozo, *The Nature of the Judicial Process* (New Haven: Yale University Press, 1921) pp. 14-23. Reprinted by permission of the publisher.

what it would have intended on a point not present to its mind, if the point had been present." . . .

. . . Sometimes the rule of constitution or of statute is clear, and then the difficulties vanish. Even when they are present, they lack at times some of that element of mystery which accompanies creative energy. We reach the land of mystery when constitution and statute are silent, and the judge must look to the common law for the rule that fits the case. He is the "living oracle of the law" in Blackstone's vivid phrase. Looking at Sir Oracle in action, viewing his work in the dry light of realism, how does he set about his task?

The first thing he does is to compare the case before him with the precedents, whether stored in his mind or hidden in the books. I do not mean that precedents are ultimate sources of the law, supplying the sole equipment that is needed for the legal armory, the sole tools, to borrow Maitland's phrase, "in the legal smithy." Back of precedents are the basic juridical conceptions which are the postulates of judicial reasoning, and farther back are the habits of life, the institutions of society, in which those conceptions had their origin, and which, by a process of interaction, they have modified in turn. Nonetheless, in a system so highly developed as our own, precedents have so covered the ground that they fix the point of departure from which the labor of the judge begins. Almost invariably, his first step is to examine and compare them. If they are plain and to the point, there may be need of nothing more. *Stare decisis* is at least the everyday working rule of our law. . . . [T]he work of deciding cases in accordance with precedents that plainly fit them is a process similar in its nature to that of deciding cases in accordance with a statute. It is a process of search, comparison, and little more. Some judges seldom get beyond that process in any case. Their notion of their duty is to match the colors of the case at hand against the colors of many sample cases spread out upon their desk. The sample nearest in shade supplies the applicable rule. But, of course, no system of living law can be evolved by such a process, and no judge of a high court, worthy of his office, views the function of his place so narrowly. If that were all there was to our calling, there would be little of intellectual interest about it. The man who had the best card index of the cases would also be the wisest judge. It is when the colors do not match, when the references in the index fail, when there is no decisive precedent, that the serious business of the judge begins. He must then fashion law for the litigants before him. In fashioning it for them, he will be fashioning it for others. . . .

. . . The rules and principles of case law have never been treated as final truths, but as working hypotheses, continually retested in those great laboratories of the law, the courts of justice. Every new case is an experiment; and if the accepted rule which seems applicable yields a result which is felt to be unjust, the rule is reconsidered. It may not be modified at once, for the attempt to do absolute justice in every single case would make the development and maintenance of general rules impossible; but if a rule continues to work injustice, it will eventually be reformulated. The principles themselves are continually retested; for if the rules derived from a principle do not work well, the principle itself must ultimately be re-examined."

CHAPTER 4

READING AND UNDERSTANDING
JUDICIAL OPINIONS

The foregoing statements by Justice Marshall, Alexander Hamilton and Justice Cardozo (in Chapter 3) help to explain why judicial opinions are critically important raw data for an analysis of the state of "the law" in a given area.

The reasoning and language in reported cases, however, is sometimes lamentably abstract. An effort to reduce a case to the simplest, most concrete, terms is a fruitful first step in understanding what is at stake. Two sorts of questions will be particularly useful:

1. What is the question before the court, and on what basis is it decided?

2. Who is the moving party and what does that party want? Although this question may seem rather simplistic, it is important to remember that litigation is expensive and burdensome. Typically, only the moving party is in court by his own choice. Therefore, one must ask: Why is this case worth the cost of initial litigation or appeal? What interest is the moving party seeking to advance? Is the moving party acting as an individual or as a representative of himself and others? Does the moving party seek to advance or defend personal interests or values, societal interests or values, or institutional interests or values?

One of the most thoughtful and informative pieces ever written on judicial case analysis is found in Professor Karl Llewellyn's, "How to Read a Case." The Llewellyn piece appears in *The Bramble Bush,** which has been required reading for generations of law students. Since "How to Read a Case" is of great use to anyone beginning the study of judicial opinions, an excerpt from the Llewellyn piece is included here for the reader's consideration:

> The first thing to do with an opinion, then, is read it. The next thing is to get clear the actual decision, the judgment rendered. Who won, the plaintiff or defendant? And watch your step here. You are after in first instance the plaintiff and defendant *below*, in the trial court. In order to follow through what happened you must therefore first know the outcome *below*; else you do not see what was appealed from, nor by whom. You now follow through

---

* Llewellyn, *The Bramble Bush, On Our Law and Its Study* (New York: Oceana Publications, 1960) pp. 41-43. Reprinted by permission of Dean Soia Mentschikoff and the publisher.

in order to see exactly what *further* judgment has been rendered on appeal. The stage is then cleared of form—although of course you do not yet know all that these forms mean, that they imply. You can turn now to what you want peculiarly to know. Given the actual judgments below and above as your indispensable framework—what has the case decided, and what can you derive from it as to what will be decided later?

You will be looking, in the opinion, or in the preliminary matter plus the opinion, for the following: a statement of the facts the court assumes; a statement of the precise way the question has come before the court—which includes what the plaintiff wanted below, and what the defendant did about it, the judgment below, and what the trial court did that is complained of; then the outcome on appeal, the judgment; and finally the reasons this court gives for doing what it did. This does not look so bad. But it is much worse than it looks.

For all our cases are decided, all our opinions are written, all our predictions, all our arguments are made, on certain four assumptions. . . .

1) *The court must decide the dispute that is before it.* It cannot refuse because the job is hard, or dubious, or dangerous.

2) *The court can decide* only *the particular dispute which is before it.* When it speaks to that question it speaks ex cathedra, with authority, with finality, with an almost magic power. When it speaks to the question before it, it announces *law*, and if what it announces is new, it legislates, it *makes* the law. But when it speaks to any other question at all, it says mere words, which no man needs to follow. Are such words worthless? They are not. We know them as judicial *dicta*; when they are wholly off the point at issue we call them *obiter dicta*—words dropped along the road, wayside remarks. Yet even wayside remarks shed light on the remarker. They may be very useful in the future to him, or to us. But he will not feel bound to them, as to his ex cathedra utterance. They came not hallowed by a Delphic frenzy. He may be slow to change them; but not so slow as in the other case.

3) *The court can decide the particular dispute only according to a* general *rule which covers a whole class of like disputes.* Our legal theory does not admit of single decisions standing on their own. If judges are free, are indeed forced, to decide new cases for which there is no rule, they must at least make a new rule as they decide. So far, good. But how wide, or how narrow, is the general rule in this particular case? That is a troublesome matter. The practice of our case-law, however, is I think fairly stated thus: it pays to be suspicious of general rules which look too wide; it pays to go slow in feeling *certain* that a wide rule has been laid

down at all, or that, if seemingly laid down, it will be followed. For there is a fourth accepted canon:

4) *Everything, everything, everything, big or small, a judge may say in an opinion, is to be read with primary reference to the particular dispute, the particular question before him.* You are not to think that the words mean what they might if they stood alone. You are to have your eye on the case in hand, and to learn how to interpret all that has been said *merely* as a reason for deciding *that* case *that* way. . . .

CHAPTER 5

STATE COURT SYSTEMS

The structure of each of the fifty state court systems is usually determined by the constitution of the individual state. While state systems may bear great resemblance to one another and to the federal system, it is important to recognize the pitfalls of overgeneralization. Every state system is a unique and independent entity—it may but it is not required to operate as others do.

Each state constitution establishes a state judicial system, including the various types of courts and judges and their powers and jurisdiction. State legislatures may be given the authority, by state constitution, to regulate the operation of the state court system. However, internal court procedures, judicial rules, and the like, are often controlled by a state judicial commission or council or by the state supreme court. In broad outline these state court systems will be familiar, but again it is essential to remember that significant variations do occur from state to state.

Many states have a three-tiered system roughly analogous to the federal structure. At the top will be a state "supreme"* court which is the ultimate arbiter on state law questions. The jurisdiction of this court will vary from state to state, depending in part whether a given state system has intermediate appellate courts as well.

At the trial level, state systems have courts of general jurisdiction and courts of special jurisdiction set up to handle litigation in defined subject areas such as probate, juvenile matters, or small claims. The subject matter jurisdiction of a state trial court may be an important threshold issue in any case where more than one forum may be appropriate.

In certain defined cases, federal and state courts may have concurrent jurisdiction over a particular claim. For example, under Section 301 of the federal Labor Management Relations Act, a union or an employer may seek enforcement of a collective bargaining agreement in either federal or state court (although federal law controls).

There are also instances when cases initiated in state court may be "removed" to federal court. As noted in Wright, Miller & Cooper, *Federal Practice and Procedure*, § 3721, Vol. 14 (West Publishing Co. 1976):

> The right to remove a case from a state to a federal court is purely statutory and therefore is entirely dependent on the will of Congress. Removal is quite an anomalous form of jurisdiction. It gives a defendant who has been sued in a state court of competent jurisdiction the right to substitute a forum of his or her own choos-

---

* The difficulty in generalizing about state systems is apparent here. In New York State, for example, the highest court is the "Court of Appeals;" the trial level court is denominated the "Supreme Court."

ing for that originally selected by the plaintiff, although the defendant's choice is extremely limited. . . . In general, an action is removable to a federal court only if it might have been brought there originally. . . .

CHAPTER 6

LEGISLATIVE AND
STATUTORY
SOURCES OF LAW

It is through the workings of the legislative branch of government that the statutes and resolutions we ordinarily conceive of as "laws" are enacted. The legislative branch of the federal government is created by the very first provision of the Constitution of the United States, Article I, Section 1, which provides that "[a]ll legislative Powers herein granted shall be vested in a Congress of the United States, which shall consist of a Senate and a House of Representatives."

The legislative process, which operates on the authority of the simple mandate of Article I, Section 1, is intricate and its workings extremely complex. The process of state lawmaking, while bearing substantial resemblance to the federal scheme outlined below, will differ from the federal model—in varying degrees—in each of the fifty jurisdictions. The following excerpt presents a capsule description of the process by which a federal law is enacted, from its origin in an idea for a legislative proposal to its ultimate publication as a federal statute:

HOW OUR LAWS ARE MADE, REPORT TO THE COMMITTEE ON THE JUDICIARY, UNITED STATES HOUSE OF REPRESENTATIVES (1978)

SOURCES OF LEGISLATION

Sources of ideas for legislation are unlimited, and proposed drafts of bills originate in many diverse quarters. First of these is, of course the idea and draft conceived by a Member himself. . . .

In addition, his constituents—either as individuals or by corporate activity such as citizen groups or associations, bar associations, labor unions, manufacturers' associations, and chambers of commerce—may avail themselves of the right to petition, which is guaranteed by the First Amendment to the Constitution, and transmit their proposals to him. Many excellent laws have originated in this way. . . .

In modern times the "executive communication" has become a prolific source of legislative proposals. This is usually in the form of a letter from a member of the President's Cabinet or the head of an independent agency—or even from the President himself—transmitting a draft of a proposed bill to the Speaker of the House of Representatives and the President of the Senate. Despite the system of separation of powers, section 3 of article II of the Constitution imposes an obligation on the President to report to the Congress from time to time on the state of the Union and to recommend for consideration such measures as he considers necessary and expedient. Many of these executive communications follow on the President's message on the state of the Union delivered to the Congress in accordance with the mandate set out in section 3 of article II of the Constitution. The communication is then referred to the standing committee having jurisdiction of the subject matter embraced in the proposal since a bill may be introduced only by a Member of Congress. The chairman of that committee usually introduces the bill promptly either in the form in which it was received or with changes he considers necessary or desirable. This practice prevails even when the majority of the House and the President are not of the same political party, although there is no constitutional or statutory requirement that a bill be introduced to effectuate the recommendations. Otherwise, the message may be considered by the committee or one of its subcommittees to determine whether a bill should be introduced. The most important of the regular executive communications is the annual message from the President transmitting the proposed budget to the Congress. This, together with testimony by officials of the various branches of the Government before the Appropriations Committees of the House and Senate, is the basis of the several appropriation bills that are drafted by the House Committee on Appropriations.

Several of the executive departments and independent agencies have staffs of trained legislative counsels whose functions include the drafting of bills to be forwarded to the Congress with a request for their enactment.

The drafting of statutes is an art that requires great skill, knowledge, and experience. In some instances a draft is the result of a study covering a period of a year or more by a commission or committee designated by the President or one of his Cabinet officers. The Administrative Procedure Act and the Uniform Code of Military Justice are only two of many examples of enactments resulting from such studies. In addition, Congressional committees sometimes draft bills after studies and hearings covering periods of a year or more. Bills to codify the laws relating to crimes and criminal procedure, the judiciary and judicial procedure, the Armed Forces, and other subjects, have each required several years of preparation. . . .

FORMS OF CONGRESSIONAL ACTION

The work of the Congress is initiated by the introduction of a proposal in one of four principal forms. These are: the bill, the joint resolution, the concurrent resolution, and the simple resolution. By far the most customary form used in both Houses is the bill. . . .

BILLS

A bill is the form used for most legislation, whether permanent or temporary, general or special, public or private.

The House of Representatives Manual prescribes the form of a House bill, as follows:

A BILL

For the establishment, etc. [as the title may be].

Be it enacted by the Senate and House of Representatives of the United States of America in Congress assembled, That, etc.

The enacting clause was prescribed by law in 1871 and is identical in all bills, whether they originate in the House of Representatives or in the Senate.

Bills may originate in either the House of Representatives or the Senate, with one notable exception provided for by the Constitution. Article I, section 7, of the Constitution, provides that all bills for raising revenue shall originate in the House of Representatives but the Senate may propose or concur with amendments, as on other bills. General appropriation bills also originate in the House of Representatives.

Article I, section 8, prescribes the matters concerning which the Congress may legislate, while section 9 of the same article places certain limitations upon Congressional action.

A bill originating in the House of Representatives is designated by the letters "H.R." followed by a number that it retains throughout all its parliamentary stages. The letters signify "House of Representatives" and not, as is sometimes supposed, "House resolution." A Senate bill is designated by the letter "S." followed by its number.

A bill that has been agreed to in identical form by both bodies becomes the law of the land only after—

    (1) Presidential approval; or

    (2) failure by the President to return it with his objections to the House in which it originated within 10 days while the Congress is in session; or

    (3) the overriding of a Presidential veto by a two-thirds vote in each House.

It does not become law without the President's signature if the Congress by their adjournment prevent its return with his objections. This is known as a "pocket veto."

JOINT RESOLUTIONS

Joint resolutions may originate either in the House of Representatives or in the Senate—not, as may be supposed, jointly in both Houses. There is little practical difference between a bill and a joint resolution and, although the latter are not as numerous as bills, the two forms are often used indiscriminately. Statutes that have been initiated as bills have later been amended by a joint resolution, and vice versa. Both are subject to the same procedure—with the exception of joint resolutions proposing an amendment to the Constitution that must be approved by two-thirds of both Houses and are then sent directly to the Administrator of General Services for submission to the several States for ratification, and that are not presented to the President for his approval.

The form of a House joint resolution is prescribed by the House of Representatives Manual, as follows:

JOINT RESOLUTION

Authorizing, etc. [as the title may be].

Resolved by the Senate and House of Representatives of the United States of America in Congress assembled, That all, etc.

The resolving clause is identical in both House and Senate joint resolutions, having been prescribed by statute in 1871. It is frequently preceded by one or more "whereas" clauses indicating the necessity for or the desirability of the joint resolution.

The term "joint" does not signify simultaneous introduction and consideration in both Houses.

A joint resolution originating in the House of Representatives is designated "H.J. Res." followed by its individual number which it retains throughout all its parliamentary stages. One originating in the Senate is designated "S.J. Res." followed by its number.

Joint resolutions become law in the same manner as bills.

CONCURRENT RESOLUTIONS

Matters affecting the operations of both Houses are usually initiated by means of concurrent resolutions. These are not normally legislative in character but are used merely for expressing facts, principles, opinions, and purposes of the two Houses. They are not equivalent to a bill and their use is narrowly limited within these bounds.

The term "concurrent" does not signify simultaneous introduction and consideration in both Houses.

A concurrent resolution originating in the House of Representatives is designated "H. Con. Res." followed by its individual number, while a Senate concurrent resolution is designated "S. Con. Res." together with its number. On approval by both Houses they are signed by the Clerk of the House and the Secretary of the Senate and transmitted to the Administrator of General Services for publication in a special part of the Statutes at Large. They are not presented to the President for action as in the cases of bills and joint resolutions unless they contain a proposition of legislation, that, of course, is not within their scope in their modern form.

SIMPLE RESOLUTIONS

A matter concerning the operation of either House alone is initiated by a simple resolution. A resolution affecting the House of Representatives is designated "H. Res." followed by its number, while a Senate resolution is designated "S. Res." together with its number. They are considered only by the body in which they were introduced and on adoption are attested to by the Clerk of the House of Representatives or the Secretary of the Senate, as the case may be, and are published in the Congressional Record.

* * *

CONSIDERATION

Our democratic tradition demands that bills be given consideration by the entire membership with adequate opportunity for debate and the proposing of amendments.

COMMITTEE OF THE WHOLE HOUSE

In order to expedite the consideration of bills and resolutions the House resorts to a parliamentary usage that enables it to act with a quorum of only 100 Members instead of the normally requisite majority, that is, 218. This consists of resolving itself into the Committee of the Whole House on the State of the Union to consider a measure. All measures on the Union Calendar—involving a tax, making appropriations, or authorizing payments out of appropriations already made—must be first considered in the Committee of the Whole. . . .

The conduct of the debate is governed principally by the standing rules of the House that are adopted at the opening of each Congress. . . . Most parliamentary questions arising during the course of debate are susceptible of ruling backed up by a precedent of action in a similar situation. The Parliamentarian of the House is present in the House Chamber in order to assist the Chairman or the Speaker in making a correct ruling on parliamentary questions.

* * *

ENGROSSMENT AND MESSAGE TO SENATE

The preparation of a copy of the bill in the form in which it has passed the House is sometimes a detailed and complicated process because of the large number and complexity of amendments to some bills adopted by the House. Frequently these amendments are offered during a spirited debate with little or no prior formal preparation. The amendment may be for the purpose of inserting new language, substituting different words for those set out in the bill, or deleting portions of the bill. It is not unusual to have more than 100 amendments, including those proposed by the committee at the time the bill is reported and those offered from the floor during the consideration of the bill in the chamber. . . . Obviously, it is extremely important that the Senate receive a copy of the bill in the precise form in which it has passed the House. The preparation of such a copy is the function of the enrolling clerk.

There is an enrolling clerk in each House, constituting a division of the office of the Clerk of the House of Representatives and of the Secretary of the Senate. He receives all the papers relating to the bill, including the official Clerk's copy of the bill as reported by the standing committee and each amendment adopted by the House. From this material he prepares the engrossed copy of the bill as passed, containing all the amendments agreed to by the House. At this point the measure ceases technically to be called a bill and is termed "an act" signifying that it is the act of one body of the Congress, although it is still popularly referred to as a bill. The engrossed bill is printed on blue paper and a certificate that it passed the House of Representatives is signed by the Clerk of the House. The engrossed bill is delivered by a reading clerk to the Senate, while that body is actually sitting, in a rather formal ceremonious manner befitting the dignity of both Houses. The reading clerk is escorted into the chamber by the Secretary or another officer of the Senate and upon being recognized by the President of the Senate states that the House has passed the bill, giving its number and title, and requests the concurrence of the Senate.

SENATE ACTION

The President of the Senate refers the engrossed bill to the appropriate standing committee of the Senate in conformity with the rules. The bill is immediately reprinted and copies are made available in the document rooms of both Houses. This printing is known as the "Act print" or the "Senate referred print."

COMMITTEE CONSIDERATION

Senate committees give the bill the same kind of detailed consideration as it received in the House, and may report it with or without amendment, or "table" it. A committee member who wishes to express his individual views, or a group of members who wish to file a minority report, may do so, if he or they give notice, at the time of the approval of the measure, of his or their intention to file supplemental, minority or additional views, in which event those views may be filed within three days with the clerk of the committee and they become a part of the report. . . .

All committee meetings, including those to conduct hearings, must be open to the public. However, a majority of the members of a committee or subcommittee may, after discussion in closed session, vote in open session to close a meeting or series of meetings on the same subject for no longer than 14 days if it is determined that the matters to be discussed or testimony to be taken will disclose matters necessary to be kept secret in the interests of national defense or the confidential conduct of the foreign relations of the United States; relate solely to internal committee staff management or procedure; tend to reflect adversely on the reputation of an individual or may represent an unwarranted invasion of privacy of the individual; may disclose law enforcement information that is required to be kept secret; may disclose certain information regarding certain trade secrets; or may disclose matters required to be kept confidential under other provisions of law or Government regulation.

CHAMBER PROCEDURE

The rules of procedure in the Senate differ to a large extent from those in the House. At the time that a bill is reported (and in the Senate this is a more formal matter than in the House of Representatives because the Senator usually announces orally that he is submitting the report) the Senator who is making the report may ask unanimous consent for the immediate consideration of the bill. If the bill is of a noncontroversial nature and there is no objection the Senate may pass the bill with little or no debate and with only a brief explanation of its purpose and effect. Even in this instance the bill is subject to amendment by any Senator. A simple majority vote is necessary to carry an amendment as well as to pass the bill. If there is any objection the report must lie over one day and the bill is placed on the calendar. . . .

When a bill has been objected to and passed over on the call of the calendar it is not necessarily lost. The majority leader, after consulting the majority policy committee of the Senate and the minority leadership, determines the time at which it will be called up for debate. At that time, a motion is made to consider the bill. The motion, which is debatable, if made after the morning hour, is sometimes the occasion for lengthy speeches, on the part of Senators opposed to the measure, intended to prevent or defeat action. This is the tactic known as "filibustering." Upon obtaining the floor Senators may speak as long as they please but may not speak more than twice on any one question in debate on the same day without leave of the Senate. Debate, however, may be closed if 16 Senators sign a motion to that effect and the motion is carried by three-fifths of the total membership of the Senate. Such a motion is voted on without debate on the second day after the day it is filed.

While a measure is being considered it is subject to amendment and each amendment, including those proposed by the committee that reported the bill, is considered separately. Generally there is no requirement that proposed amendments be germane to the subject matter of the bill except in the case of general appropriation bills. Under the rules of the Senate a "rider," that is, an amendment proposing substantive legislation to an appropriation bill is prohibited, but this prohibition may be suspended by two-thirds vote on a motion to permit consideration of such an amendment on one day's notice in writing. Debate on the measure must be germane during the first three hours after the morning hour unless determined to the contrary by unanimous consent or on motion without debate. After final action on the amendments the bill is ready for engrossment and the third reading, which is usually by title only, although if demanded, it must be read in full. The Presiding Officer then puts the question on the passage and the vote is usually taken viva voce although a yea-and-nay vote is in order if demanded by one-fifth of the Senators present. A simple majority is necessary for passage. Before an amended measure is cleared for its return to the House of Representatives (or an unamended measure is cleared for enrollment) a Senator who voted with the prevailing side, or who abstained from voting, may make a motion within the next two days to reconsider the action. If the measure was passed without a recorded vote, any Senator may make the motion to reconsider. That motion is usually tabled and its tabling constitutes a final determination. If, however, the motion is granted, the Senate, by majority vote, may either affirm its action, which then becomes final, or reverse it.

The original engrossed House bill, together with the engrossed Senate amendments, if any, is then returned to the House with a message stating the action taken by the Senate. Where amendments have been made by the Senate the message requests that the House concur in them.

FINAL ACTION ON AMENDED BILL

On their return to the House the official papers relating to the amended measure are placed on the Speaker's table to await House action on the Senate amendments. If amendments are of a minor or noncontroversial nature the Chairman of the committee that originally reported the bill—or any Member—may, at the direction of the committee, ask unanimous consent to take the bill with the amendments from the Speaker's table and agree to the Senate amendments. At this point the Clerk reads the title of the bill and the Senate amendments. If there is no objection the amendments are then declared to be agreed to, and the bill is ready to be enrolled for presentation to the President. Lacking unanimous consent, bills that do not require consideration in the Committee of the Whole are privileged and may be called up from the Speaker's table by motion for immediate consideration of the amendments. A simple majority is necessary to carry the motion and thereby complete floor action on the measure. A Senate amendment to a House bill is subject to a point of order that it must first be considered in the Committee of the Whole, if, originating in the House, it would be subject to that point.

REQUEST FOR A CONFERENCE

If, however, the amendments are substantial or controversial the Member may request unanimous consent to take the bill with the Senate amendments from the Speaker's table, disagree to the amendments and request a conference with the Senate to resolve the disagreeing votes of the two Houses. . . ,

The conference committee is sometimes popularly referred to as the "Third House of Congress". . . .

The conferees are strictly limited in their consideration to matters in disagreement between the two Houses. Consequently they may not strike out or amend any portion of the bill that was not amended by the Senate. Furthermore, they may not insert new matter that is not germane to the differences between the two Houses. . . .

CONFERENCE REPORTS

When the conferees, by majority vote of each group, have reached complete agreement (or find that they are able to agree with respect to some but not all amendments) they embody their recommendations in a report made in duplicate that must be signed by a majority of the conferees appointed by each body. . . .

The report is required to be printed in both Houses and must be accompanied by an explanatory statement prepared jointly by the conferees on the part of the House and the conferees on the part of the Senate. The statement must be sufficiently detailed and explicit to inform the Congress as to the effect that the amendments or propositions contained in the report will have on the measure to which those amendments or propositions relate. The engrossed bill and amendments and one copy of the report are delivered to the body that is to act first on the report; namely, the body that had agreed to the conference requested by the other. . . .

A report that contains any recommendations which go beyond the differences between the two Houses is subject to a point of order in its entirety. Any change in the text as agreed to by both Houses renders the report subject to the point of order and the matter is before the House *de novo*.

* * *

ENROLLMENT

When the bill has been agreed to in identical form by both bodies—either without amendment by the Senate, or by House concurrence in the Senate amendments, or by agreement in both bodies to the conference report—a copy of the bill is enrolled for presentation to the President.

The preparation of the enrolled bill is a painstaking and important task since it must reflect precisely the effect of all amendments, either by way of deletion, substitution, or addition, agreed to by both bodies. The enrolling clerk of the House (with respect to bills originating in the House) receives the original engrossed bill, the engrossed Senate amendments, the signed conference report, the several messages from the Senate, and a notation of the final action by the House, for the purpose of preparing the enrolled copy. From these he must prepare meticulously the final form of the bill, as it was agreed to by both Houses, for presentation to the President. On occasion there have been upward of 500 amendments, particularly after a conference, each of which must be set out in the enrollment exactly as agreed to, and all punctuation must be in accord with the action taken.

The enrolled bill is printed on parchment paper, with a certificate on the reverse side of the last page, to be signed by the Clerk of the House stating that the bill originated in the House of Representatives (or by the Secretary of the Senate when the bill has originated in that body). It is examined for accuracy by the Committee on House Administration (or by the Secretary of the Senate when the bill originated in that body). When the Committee is satisfied with the accuracy of the bill the Chairman of the Committee attaches a slip stating that it finds the bill truly enrolled and sends it to the Speaker of the House for his signature. All bills, regardless of the body in which they originated, are signed first by the Speaker and then by the President of the Senate. The Speaker and the President of the Senate may sign bills only while their respective House is actually sitting unless advance permission is granted to them to sign during a recess or after adjournment. After both signatures are affixed the bill is returned to the Committee for the purpose of being presented to the President for his action under the Constitution.

PRESIDENTIAL ACTION

The Constitution provides that—

Every Bill which shall have passed the House of Representatives and the Senate, shall, before it becomes a Law, be presented to the President of the United States.

In actual practice a clerk of the Committee on House Administration (or the Secretary of the Senate when the bill originated in that body) delivers the original enrolled bill to an employee at the White House and obtains a receipt, and the fact of the delivery is then reported to the House by the Chairman of the Committee. Delivery to a White House employee has customarily been regarded as presentation to the President and as commencing the 10-day Constitutional period for Presidential action.

Copies of the enrolled bill are usually transmitted by the White House to the various departments interested in the subject matter so that they may advise the President who, of course, cannot be personally familiar with every item in every bill.

If the President approves the bill he signs it and usually writes the word "approved" and the date, the only Constitutional requirement being that he sign it.

The Supreme Court has stated that undoubtedly the President when approving bills may be said to participate in the enactment of laws, which the Constitution requires him to execute.

The bill may become law without the President's signature by virtue of the Constitutional provision that if he does not return a bill with his objections within 10 days (Sundays excepted) after it has been presented to him, it shall be a law in like manner as if he had signed it. However, if the Congress by their adjournment prevent its return, it does not become law. The latter event is what is known as a "pocket veto," that is, the bill does not become law even though the President has not sent his objections to the Congress.

Notice of the signing of a bill by the President is usually sent by message to the House in which it originated and that House informs the other, although this action is not necessary to the validity of the act. The action is also noted in the Congressional Record.

A bill becomes law on the date of approval (or passage over the President's veto), unless it expressly provides a different effective date.

VETO MESSAGE

By the terms of the Constitution, if the President does not approve the bill "he shall return it, with his objections to that House in which it shall have originated, who shall enter the objections at large on their Journal, and proceed to reconsider it." It is the usual but not invariable rule that a bill returned with the President's objections must be voted on at once and when laid before the House the question on the passage is considered as pending. A vetoed bill is always privileged, and a motion to take it from the table is in order at any time.

The Member in charge moves the previous question which is put by the Speaker, as follows: "The question is, Will the House on reconsideration agree to pass the bill, the objections of the President to the contrary notwithstanding?" The Clerk calls the roll and those in favor of passing the bill answer "Aye," and those opposed "No." If fewer than two-thirds of the Members present (constituting a quorum) vote in the affirmative the bill is killed, and a message is usually sent to the Senate advising that body of the decision that the bill shall not pass. If, however, two-thirds vote in the affirmative, the bill is sent with the President's objections to the Senate together with a message advising it of the action in the House.

There is a similar procedure in the Senate where again a two-thirds affirmative vote is necessary to pass the bill over the President's objections. If then passed by the Senate the measure becomes the law of the land notwithstanding the objections of the President, and it is ready for publication as a binding statute.

PUBLICATION

One of the important steps in the enactment of a valid law is the requirement that it shall be made known to the people who are to be bound by it. Obviously, there would be no justice if the state were to hold its people responsible for their conduct before it made known to them the unlawfulness of such behavior. That idea is implicit in the Constitutional prohibition against enacting *ex post facto* laws. In practice, our laws are published immediately upon their enactment so that they may be known to the people.

If the President approves a bill, or allows it to become law without his signature, the original enrolled bill is sent from the White House to the Administrator of General Services for publication. If a bill is passed by both Houses over the objections of the President the body that last overrides the veto likewise transmits it. There it is assigned a public law number, and paginated for the Statutes at Large volume covering that session of the Congress. The public law numbers run in sequence starting anew at the beginning of each Congress, and since 1957 are prefixed for ready identification by the number of the Congress—e.g., the first public law of the 95th Congress is designated Public Law 95-1 and subsequent laws of this Congress will also contain the same prefix designator.

"SLIP LAWS"

The first official publication of the statute is in the form generally known as the "slip law." In this form, each law is published separately as an unbound pamphlet. Since the beginning of the 82d Congress, in 1951, the slip laws have been printed by photo-electric offset process from the original enrolled bill. This process ensures accuracy and saves both time and expense in preparing the copy. A heading indicates the public law number and bill number, and the date of approval. If the statute has been passed over the veto of the President, or has become law without his signature because he did not return it with his objections, an appropriate statement is inserted in lieu of the usual notation of approval. . . .

Copies of the slip laws are delivered to the document rooms of both Houses where they become available to officials and the public immediately. They may also be obtained by annual subscription or individual purchase from the Superintendent of Documents at the Government Printing Office. . . .

STATUTES AT LARGE

For the purpose of providing a permanent collection of the laws of each session of the Congress the bound volumes, which are called the United States Statutes at Large, are prepared by the General Services Administration. When the latest volume containing the laws of the first session of the 95th Congress becomes available it will be No. 91 in the series. Each volume contains a complete index and a table of contents and, since 1956, a table of earlier laws affected, as well as a most useful table showing the legislative history of each law in the volume. There are also extensive marginal notes referring to laws in earlier volumes and earlier and later matters in the same volume.

Under the provisions of a statute originally enacted in 1895 these volumes are legal evidence of the laws contained in them and will be accepted as proof of those laws in any court in the United States.

The Statutes at Large are only a chronological arrangement of the laws exactly as they have been enacted. There is no attempt to arrange the laws according to their subject matter or to show the present status of an earlier law that has been amended on one or more occasions. That is the function of a code of laws.

UNITED STATES CODE

The United States Code contains a consolidation and codification of the general and permanent laws of the United States arranged according to subject matter under fifty title headings, in alphabetical order to a large degree. It sets out the current status of the laws, as amended, without repeating all the language of the amendatory acts except where necessary for that purpose and is declared to be prima facie evidence of those laws. Its purpose is to present the laws in a concise and usable form without requiring recourse to the many volumes of the Statutes at Large containing the individual amendments.

The Code is prepared by the Law Revision Counsel of the House of Representatives. New editions are published every six years and cumulative supplements are published after the conclusion of each regular session of the Congress.

CHAPTER 7

ADMINISTRATIVE RULES
AND REGULATIONS
AS SOURCES OF LAW

1. *Federal Administrative Law*

While it is undisputed that Congress is empowered to delegate the legislative power necessary for administrative agencies to implement its policies and programs, the notion remains that Congress should limit the discretion it vests in those agencies by precise legislative formulation of its directives to them. Various statements of the so-called "non-delegation doctrine" stand for the proposition that where the legislature specifies in detail the policies to be followed by administrators, agencies will be properly limited to "filling in the details" of congressional directives.

As a practical matter, however, congressional delegations to administrative authorities are routinely upheld in cases even where standards of clear statement are not met. Congress, whether by design or inaction, often fails to define intelligible standards or governing principles to guide subordinate agencies in their work. And despite an initial lack of direction, a body of agency law does evolve over time, as the "expert" agencies define problems, make policy and apply standards to particular cases.

The hundreds of volumes of the Code of Federal Regulations contain rules made by federal agencies pursuant to the *rulemaking* power delegated to them by Congress; agency case law demonstrates the *adjudicatory* power by virtue of which questions of policy are elaborated and individual disputes resolved on a case-by-case basis. If the federal Administrative Procedure Act (APA), 5 U.S.C. § 551 *et seq.*, were to be read literally, it would appear that by defining "adjudication" as a process for a final disposition in a matter other than "rulemaking," the APA limits all administrative action to either adjudication or rulemaking. Yet, as commentators in the field of administrative law are quick to recognize, in reality only a tiny proportion of routine agency action fits within these formal statutory categorizations:

> Agencies do not necessarily either adjudicate or make rules when they initiate, investigate, threaten, publicize, conceal, plan, recommend, and supervise. Some informal action of agencies is in the nature of informal adjudication, and some is in the nature of informal rulemaking, but the general understanding continues that some informal action is neither adjudication nor rulemaking.[1]

---

[1] Davis, *Administrative Law Treatise*, 2d ed., Vol. 1, § 1:4 (San Diego: K.C. Davis Publishing Co., 1978) pp. 13-14.

As Professor Davis observes, one measure of the importance of this informal action is its quantity. He estimates that "more than ninety percent of all administrative action is informal." [2]

Predictably, individuals and institutions subject to the expanding power of the federal regulatory machine, resort to judicial review as an instrument for checking executive and independent agency governmental power. Whether "formal" or "informal," agency rules and decisions viewed as unwarranted incursions on protected private interests are increasingly subject to challenge in the federal courts.

The traditional model of American administrative law is one in which judicial review operates as the mechanism for control of official intrusions on private interests. The focus of this review historically has been twofold: on whether administrative discretion has been exercised within statutorily authorized bounds and on whether agency procedures have been adequate to insure the accuracy, rationality and reviewability of agency implementation of legislative directives. Legislative and judicial controls aimed at protecting individuals and regulated entities from the arbitrary exercise of agency discretion were thought sufficient guarantees that agencies would act to advance the "public interest."

Students of administrative law in the nineteen-sixties and seventies have witnessed the gradual erosion of the traditional model and the assumptions and compromises it entailed.[3] Public confidence that legislative and judicial controls would create agencies equipped to act in the public interest is a thing of the past. Some critics now claim that agencies are mere "captives" of regulated entities and, therefore, that the agencies are unable to protect the public interest pursuant to objective bases for social choice, a fundamental tenet of the traditional model. As Professor Stewart explains, some critics have come to "doubt the very existence of an ascertainable national welfare as a meaningful guide to administrative decision." [4] As a result, the function of agencies can no longer be conceptualized simply as that of putting broad legislative directives into practice:

> Today the exercise of agency discretion is inevitably seen as the essentially legislative practice of adjusting the competing claims of various private interests affected by agency policy. The unravelling of the notion of an objective goal for administration is reflected in statements by judges and legal commentators that the "public interest is a texture of multiple strands," that it "is not monolith," and "involves a balance of many interests." Courts have asserted that agencies must consider all of the various interests affected by their decisions as an essential predicate to "balancing

---

[2] *Id.*

[3] *See generally,* Stewart, *The Reformation of American Administrative Law,* 88 Harv. L. Rev. 1669 (1975).

[4] *Id.* at 1683. *See also,* ABA Commission on Law and the Economy, *Federal Regulation: Roads to Reform* (Chicago: American Bar Association, 1979).

all elements essential to a just determination of the public interest." [5]

During a period of contemporary history that has witnessed a virtual explosion of governmental involvement in many spheres of American life, the need for adequate representation of individuals and institutions affected by agency decisions has come to be recognized. Political, social and industrial entities are affected by federal regulation of the economy, the environment and multiple facets of the employment relationship. At the same time, individuals increasingly look to the federal government as a provider of goods, services and employment.

The traditional model of administrative law has been stretched, if not transformed, in attempting to respond to and control this increase in governmental power. Professor Stewart outlines four doctrinal developments through which control of administrative action has been extended:

(1) The establishment of an increasingly strong presumption of judicial review of agency action (or inaction);

(2) The enlargement of the class of interests entitled under the due process clause to an administrative hearing before agency infringement of those interests;

(3) The enlargement of the class of interests entitled by statute or regulation to participate in formal processes of agency decision;

(4) The enlargement of the class of interests entitled to obtain judicial review of agency action. [6]

Nevertheless, the reader should understand that it is difficult, if not impossible, to generalize about the current state of "administrative law" in the United States. Much of what an agency can do is defined by statute and subject to judicial review. A number of laws which state the missions of various federal agencies (such as the Federal Trade Commission) are currently under review. In addition, in *Vermont Yankee Nuclear Power Corp. v. National Resources Defense Council*, 435 U.S. 519 (1978), the United States Supreme Court called into question the role of the courts in formulating procedures before administrative agencies. "An oversimplified statement of the case is that the Supreme Court forbade lower courts to add to the procedural requirements of § 553 of the Administrative Procedure Act" [7] when reviewing the legitimacy of an agency action.

The main point is that, although federal "administrative" rules and regulations are important sources of law affecting academic institutions, the law in this area is always in a state of flux. For further references on this subject, the reader should consult the bibliography in Appendix A.

---

[5] *Id.*

[6] *Id.* at 1716.

[7] Davis, *1980 Supplement to Administrative Law Treatise*, § 8.03 (San Diego: K.C. Davis Pub. Co., 1980). The *Vermont Yankee* decision is discussed at length, and severely criticized by Prof. Davis at §§ 6.35-6.37.

2. State Administrative Law

Institutions of higher education will, to varying degrees, be regulated by administrative agencies, boards or commissions in their home states. Matters such as public education, zoning, licensing and utilities regulation are typical subjects of state and local control; others, such as equal employment opportunity, environmental protection and workplace safety often are the subject of overlapping regulations by state and federal entities. The central concerns of an entity or individual subject to state administrative action will be analogous to those of one faced with regulation in the federal sphere: for example, whether rulemaking has been accompanied by notice to interested persons and the opportunity to submit views or information; whether administrative rules are adequately publicized; and whether parties are afforded appropriate procedural protection in the conduct of adjudicatory proceedings. If Professor Davis' estimate of the prevalence of "informal" action applies at the state level as well, the regulatee's most crucial operational concern will be the predictability and perceived reasonableness of such informal action.

While it is possible to generalize about "issues" in state administrative law, generalization about the laws themselves is here mostly a matter of academic interest. Each of the fifty state jurisdictions must be viewed separately to determine substantive and procedural regulations within a given state.

APPENDIX A

BIBLIOGRAPHY

BIBLIOGRAPHY

Alexander and Solomon, College and University Law (Charlottesville: The Michie Company, 1972).

Alexander, K., School Law (St. Paul: West Publishing Co., 1980).

Auerbach, C., Garrison, L., Hurst, W., and Mermin, S., The Legal Process (San Francisco: Chandler Publishing Co., 1961).

Cardozo, B., The Nature of the Judicial Process (New Haven: Yale University Press, 1921).

Choper, J., Kamisar, Y., Tribe, L., The Supreme Court: Trends & Developments, 1978-79 (Minneapolis: National Practice Institute, Inc., 1979).

Commission on Law and the Economy, American Bar Association, Federal Regulation: Roads to Reform (Chicago: American Bar Association, 1979).

Davis, K., Administrative Law Treatise, 2d ed., Vol. 1 (San Diego: K.C. Davis Pub. Co., 1978).

Davis, K., Administrative Law Treatise, 2d ed., Vol. 2 (San Diego: K.C. Davis Pub. Co., 1979).

Friedman, L., A History of American Law (New York: Simon & Schuster, 1973).

Friendly, H., Federal Jurisdiction: A General View (New York and London: Columbia University Press, 1973).

Gunther, G., Cases and Materials on Constitutional Law (Mineola, N.Y.: The Foundation Press, Inc.).

Hollander, P., Legal Handbook for Educators (Boulder, Colo.: Westview Press, 1978).

Hudgins, H.C. and Vacca, R.S., Law and Education: Contemporary Issues and Court Decisions (Charlottesville: The Michie Co., 1979).

Hurst, J., The Growth of American Law: The Law Makers (Boston: Little, Brown & Co., 1950).

Jones, H., ed., The Courts, the Public and The Law Explosion (Englewood Cliffs, N.J.: Prentice Hall, 1965).

Kaplin, W., The Law of Higher Education (San Francisco: Jossey-Bass Publishers, 1978).

Llewellyn, K., The Bramble Bush (Dobbs Ferry, N.Y.: Oceana Publications, Inc., 1930).

Lockhart, Kamisar & Choper, Constitutional Law (St. Paul: West Publishing Company).

McGowan, C., The Organization of Judicial Power in the United States (Evanston, Ill.: Northwestern Univ. Press 1969).

Morris, A., The Constitution and American Education, 2d ed. (St. Paul: West Publishing Company, 1979).

Rombauer, M., Legal Problem Solving (St. Paul: West Publishing Company, 1978).

Schwartz, B., Constitutional Law: A Textbook, 2d ed. (New York: Mac-Millan Publishing Co., Inc., 1979).

Schwartz, B., Law in America: A History (New York: McGraw-Hill Book Co., 1974).

The Supreme Court: Justice and the Law, 2d ed. (Washington, D.C.: Congressional Quarterly, Inc., 1977).

Tribe, L. American Constitutional Law (Mineola, N.Y.: The Foundation Press).

Zinn, C., How Our Laws Are Made, revised by E. Willett, Report to the Committee on the Judiciary, United States House of Representatives (1978).

APPENDIX B

THE UNITED STATES CONSTITUTION

THE CONSTITUTION OF THE UNITED STATES OF AMERICA

We the people of the United States, in Order to form a more perfect Union, establish Justice, insure domestic Tranquility, provide for the common defence, promote the general Welfare, and secure the Blessings of Liberty to ourselves and our Posterity, do ordain and establish this Constitution for the United States of America.

ARTICLE I

SECTION 1. All legislative Powers herein granted shall be vested in a Congress of the United States, which shall consist of a Senate and House of Representatives.

SECTION 2. The House of Representatives shall be composed of Members chosen every second Year by the People of the several States, and the Electors in each State shall have the Qualifications requisite for Electors of the most numerous Branch of the State Legislature.

No person shall be a Representative who shall not have attained to the Age of twenty-five Years, and been seven Years a Citizen of the United States, and who shall not, when elected, be an Inhabitant of that State in which he shall be chosen.

Representatives and direct Taxes shall be apportioned among the several States which may be included within this Union, according to their respective Numbers, which shall be determined by adding to the whole Number of free Persons, including those bound to Service for a Term of Years, and excluding Indians not taxed, three fifths of all other Persons. The actual Enumeration shall be made within three Years after the first Meeting of the Congress of the United States, and within every subsequent Term of ten Years, in such Manner as they shall by Law direct. The Number of Representatives shall not exceed one for every thirty Thousand, but each State shall have at Least one Representative; and until such enumeration shall be made, the State of New Hampshire shall be entitled to chuse three, Massachusetts eight, Rhode Island and Providence Plantations one, Connecticut five, New York six, New Jersey four, Pennsylvania eight, Delaware one, Maryland six, Virginia ten, North Carolina five, South Carolina five, and Georgia three.

When vacancies happen in the Representation from any State, the Executive Authority thereof shall issue Writs of Election to fill such Vacancies.

The House of Representatives shall chuse their Speaker and other Officers; and shall have the sole Power of Impeachment.

SECTION 3. The Senate of the United States shall be composed of two Senators from each State, chosen by the Legislature thereof, for six Years; and each Senator shall have one Vote.

Immediately after they shall be assembled in Consequence of the first Election, they shall be divided as equally as may be into three Classes. The Seats of the Senators of the first Class shall be vacated at the Expiration of the second Year, of the second Class at the Expiration of the fourth Year, and of the third Class at the Expiration of the sixth Year, so that one third may be chosen every second Year; and if Vacancies happen by Resignation, or otherwise, during the Recess of the Legislature of any State, the Executive thereof may make temporary Appointments until the next Meeting of the Legislature, which shall then fill such Vacancies.

No Person shall be a Senator who shall not have attained to the Age of thirty Years, and been nine Years a Citizen of the United States, and who shall not, when elected, be an Inhabitant of that State for which he shall be chosen.

The Vice President of the United States shall be President of the Senate, but shall have no Vote, unless they be equally divided.

The Senate shall chuse their other Officers, and also a President pro tempore, in the absence of the Vice President, or when he shall exercise the Office of President of the United States.

The Senate shall have the sole Power to try all Impeachments. When sitting for that Purpose, they shall be on Oath or Affirmation. When the President of the United States is tried, the Chief Justice shall preside: And no Person shall be convicted without the Concurrence of two thirds of the Members present.

Judgment in Cases of Impeachment shall not extend further than to removal from Office, and disqualification to hold and enjoy any Office of honor, Trust or Profit under the United States: but the Party convicted shall nevertheless be liable and subject to Indictment, Trial, Judgment and Punishment, according to Law.

SECTION 4. The Times, Places and Manner of holding Elections for Senators and Representatives, shall be prescribed in each State by the Legislature thereof; but the Congress may at any time by Law make or alter such Regulations, except as to the Places of Chusing Senators.

The Congress shall assemble at least once in every Year, and such Meeting shall be on the first Monday in December, unless they shall by Law appoint a different Day.

SECTION 5. Each House shall be the Judge of the Elections, Returns and Qualifications of its own Members, and a Majority of each shall constitute a Quorum to do Business; but a smaller Number may adjourn from day to day, and may be authorized to compel the Attendance of absent Members, in such Manner, and under such Penalties as each House may provide.

Each House may determine the Rules of its Proceedings, punish its Members for disorderly Behavior, and, with the Concurrence of two thirds, expel a Member.

Each House shall keep a Journal of its Proceedings, and from time to time publish the same, excepting such Parts as may in their Judgment require Secrecy; and the Yeas and Nays of the Members of either House on any question shall, at the Desire of one fifth of those Present, be entered on the journal.

Neither House, during the Session of Congress, shall, without the Consent of the other, adjourn for more than three days, nor to any other Place than that in which the two Houses shall be sitting.

SECTION 6. The Senators and Representatives shall receive a Compensation for their Services, to be ascertained by Law, and paid out of the Treasury of the United States. They shall in all Cases, except Treason, Felony and Breach of the Peace, be privileged from Arrest during their Attendance at the Session of their respective Houses, and in going to and returning from the same; and for any Speech or Debate in either House, they shall not be questioned in any other Place.

No Senator or Representative shall, during the Time for which he was elected, be appointed to any civil Office under the Authority of the United States, which shall have been created, or the Emoluments whereof shall have been encreased during such time; and no Person holding any Office under the United States, shall be a Member of either House during his Continuance in Office.

SECTION 7. All Bills for raising Revenue shall originate in the House of Representatives; but the Senate may propose or concur with Amendments as on other Bills.

Every Bill which shall have passed the House of Representatives and the Senate, shall, before it become a Law, be presented to the President of the United States; If he approve he shall sign it, but if not he shall return it, with his Objections to that House in which it shall have originated, who shall enter the Objections at large on their Journal, and proceed to reconsider it. If after such Reconsideration two thirds of that House shall agree to pass the Bill, it shall be sent, together with the Objections, to the other House, by which it shall likewise be reconsidered, and if approved by two thirds of that House, it shall become a Law. But in all such Cases the Votes of both Houses shall be determined by Yeas and Nays, and the Names of the Persons voting for and against the Bill shall be entered on the Journal of each House respectively. If any Bill shall not be returned by the President within ten Days (Sundays excepted) after it shall have been presented to him, the Same shall be a Law, in like Manner as if he had signed it, unless the Congress by their Adjournment prevent its Return, in which Case it shall not be a Law.

Every Order, Resolution, or Vote to which the Concurrence of the Senate and House of Representatives may be necessary (except on a question of Adjournment) shall be presented to the President of the United States;

and before the Same shall take Effect, shall be approved by him, or being disapproved by him, shall be repassed by two thirds of the Senate and House of Representatives, according to the Rules and Limitations prescribed in the Case of a Bill.

SECTION 8.   The Congress shall have Power To lay and collect Taxes, Duties, Imposts and Excises, to pay the Debts and provide for the common Defence and general Welfare of the United States; but all Duties, Imposts and Excises shall be uniform throughout the United States;

To borrow Money on the Credit of the United States;

To regulate Commerce with foreign Nations, and among the several States, and with the Indian Tribes;

To establish an uniform Rule of Naturalization, and uniform Laws on the subject of Bankruptcies throughout the United States;

To coin Money, regulate the Value thereof, and of foreign Coin, and fix the Standard of Weights and Measures;

To provide for the Punishment of counterfeiting the Securities and current Coin of the United States;

To establish Post Offices and post Roads;

To promote the Progress of Science and useful Arts, by securing for limited Times to Authors and Inventors the exclusive Right to their respective Writings and Discoveries;

To constitute Tribunals inferior to the supreme Court;

To define and punish Piracies and Felonies committed on the high Seas, and Offenses against the Law of Nations;

To declare War, grant Letters of Marque and Reprisal, and make Rules concerning Captures on Land and Water;

To raise and support Armies, but no Appropriation of Money to that Use shall be for a longer Term than two Years;

To provide and maintain a Navy;

To make Rules for the Government and Regulation of the land and naval Forces;

To provide for calling forth the Militia to execute the Laws of the Unions, suppress Insurrections and repel Invasions;

To provide for organizing, arming, and disciplining the Militia, and for governing such Part of them as may be employed in the Service of the United States, reserving to the States respectively, the Appointment of the Officers, and the Authority of training the Militia according to the discipline prescribed by Congress.

To exercise exclusive Legislation in all Cases whatsoever, over such District (not exceeding ten Miles square) as may, by Cession of particular States, and the acceptance of Congress, become the Seat of the Government of the United States, and to exercise like Authority over all Places purchased by the Consent of the Legislature of the State in which the Same shall be, for the Erection of Forts, Magazines, Arsenals, dock-Yards, and other needful Buildings;—And

To make all Laws which shall be necessary and proper for carrying into Execution the foregoing Powers, and all other Powers vested by this Constitution in the Government of the United States, or in any Department or Officer thereof.

SECTION 9. The Migration or Importation of such Persons as any of the States now existing shall think proper to admit, shall not be prohibited by the Congress prior to the Year one thousand eight hundred and eight, but a Tax or duty may be imposed on such Importation, not exceeding ten dollars for each Person.

The privilege of the Writ of Habeas Corpus shall not be suspended, unless when in Cases of Rebellion or Invasion the public Safety may require it.

No Bill of Attainder or ex post facto Law shall be passed.

No capitation, or other direct, Tax shall be laid, unless in Proportion to the Census or Enumeration herein before directed to be taken.

No Tax or Duty shall be laid on Articles exported from any State.

No Preference shall be given by any Regulation of Commerce or Revenue to the Ports of one State over those of another; nor shall Vessels bound to, or from, one State, be obliged to enter, clear, or pay Duties in another.

No Money shall be drawn from the Treasury, but in Consequence of Appropriations made by Law; and a regular Statement and Account of the Receipts and Expenditures of all public Money shall be published from time to time.

No Title of Nobility shall be granted by the United States: And no Person holding any Office of Profit or Trust under them, shall, without the Consent of the Congress, accept of any present, Emolument, Office, or Title, of any kind whatever, from any King, Prince, or foreign State.

SECTION 10. No State shall enter into any Treaty, Alliance, or Confederation; grant Letters of Marque and Reprisal; coin Money; emit Bills of Credit; make any Thing but gold and silver Coin a Tender in Payment of Debts; pass any Bill of Attainder, ex post facto Law, or Law impairing the Obligation of Contracts, or grant any Title of Nobility.

No State shall, without the Consent of the Congress, lay any Imposts or Duties on Imports or Exports, except what may be absolutely necessary for executing its inspection Laws: and the net Produce of all Duties and Imposts, laid by any State on Imports or Exports, shall be for the Use of the Treasury of the United States; and all such Laws shall be subject to the Revision and Controul of the Congress.

No State shall, without the Consent of Congress, lay any duty of Tonnage, keep Troops, or Ships of War in time of Peace, enter into any Agreement or Compact with another State, or with a foreign Power, or engage in War, unless actually invaded, or in such imminent Danger as will not admit of delay.

ARTICLE II

SECTION 1. The executive Power shall be vested in a President of the United States of America. He shall hold his Office during the Term of four Years, and, together with the Vice President, chosen for the same Term, be elected, as follows

Each State shall appoint, in such Manner as the Legislature thereof may direct, a Number of Electors, equal to the whole Number of Senators and Representatives to which the State may be entitled in the Congress: but no Senator or Representative, or Person holding an Office of Trust or Profit under the United States, shall be appointed an Elector.

The Electors shall meet in their respective States, and vote by Ballot for two persons, of whom one at least shall not be an Inhabitant of the same State with themselves. And they shall make a List of all the Persons voted for, and of the Number of Votes for each; which List they shall sign and certify, and transmit sealed to the Seat of the Government of the United States, directed to the President of the Senate. The President of the Senate shall, in the Presence of the Senate and House of Representatives, open all the Certificates, and the Votes shall then be counted. The Person having the greatest Number of Votes shall be the President, if such Number be a Majority of the whole Number of Electors appointed; and if there be more than one who have such Majority, and have an equal Number of Votes, then the House of Representatives shall immediately chuse by Ballot one of them for President; and if no Person have a Majority, then from the five highest on the List the said House shall in like Manner chuse the President. But in chusing the President, the Votes shall be taken by States, the Representation from each State having one Vote; A quorum for this Purpose shall consist of a Member or Members from two thirds of the States, and a Majority of all the States shall be necessary to a Choice. In every Case, after the Choice of the President, the Person having the greatest Number of Votes of Electors shall be the Vice President. But if there should remain two or more who have equal Votes, the Senate shall chuse from them by Ballot the Vice President.

The Congress may determine the Time of chusing the Electors, and the Day on which they shall give their Votes; which Day shall be the same throughout the United States.

No person except a natural born Citizen, or a Citizen of the United States, at the time of the Adoption of this Constitution, shall be eligible to the Office of President; neither shall any Person be eligible to that Office who shall not have attained to the Age of thirty-five Years, and been fourteen Years a Resident within the United States.

In Case of the Removal of the President from Office, or of his Death, Resignation, or Inability to discharge the Powers and Duties of the said Office, the same shall devolve on the Vice President, and the Congress may by Law provide for the Case of Removal, Death, Resignation or Inability, both of the President and Vice President, declaring what Officer shall then act as

President, and such Officer shall act accordingly, until the Disability be removed, or a President shall be elected.

The President shall, at stated Times, receive for his Services, a Compensation, which shall neither be encreased nor diminished during the Period for which he shall have been elected, and he shall not receive within that Period any other Emolument from the United States, or any of them.

Before he enter on the Execution of his Office, he shall take the following Oath or Affirmation: "I do solemnly swear (or affirm) that I will faithfully execute the Office of President of the United States, and will to the best of my Ability, preserve, protect and defend the Constitution of the United States."

SECTION 2. The President shall be Commander in Chief of the Army and Navy of the United States, and of the Militia of the several States, when called into the actual Service of the United States; he may require the Opinion in writing, of the principal Officer in each of the executive Departments, upon any subject relating to the Duties of their respective Offices, and he shall have Power to Grant Reprieves and Pardons for Offenses against the United States, except in Cases of Impeachment.

He shall have Power, by and with the Advice and Consent of the Senate, to make Treaties, provided two thirds of the Senators present concur; and he shall nominate, and by and with the Advice and Consent of the Senate, shall appoint Ambassadors, other public Ministers and Consuls, Judges of the supreme Court, and all other Officers of the United States, whose Appointments are not herein otherwise provided for, and which shall be established by Law: but the Congress may by Law vest the Appointment of such inferior Officers, as they think proper, in the President alone, in the Courts of Law, or in the Heads of Departments.

The President shall have Power to fill up all Vacancies that may happen during the Recess of the Senate, by granting Commissions which shall expire at the End of their next Session.

SECTION 3. He shall from time to time give to the Congress Information of the State of the Union, and recommend to their Consideration such Measures as he shall judge necessary and expedient; he may, on extraordinary Occasions, convene both Houses, or either of them, and in Case of Disagreement between them, with Respect to the Time of Adjournment, he may adjourn them to such Time as he shall think proper; he shall receive Ambassadors and other public Ministers; he shall take Care that the Laws be faithfully executed, and shall Commission all the Officers of the United States.

SECTION 4. The President, Vice President and all civil Officers of the United States, shall be removed from Office on Impeachment for, and Conviction of, Treason, Bribery, or other high Crimes and Misdemeanors.

ARTICLE III

SECTION 1. The judicial Power of the United States, shall be vested in one supreme Court, and in such inferior Courts as the Congress may from time to time ordain and establish. The Judges, both of the supreme and inferior Courts, shall hold their Offices during good Behaviour, and shall, at stated Times, receive for their Services a Compensation which shall not be diminished during their Continuance in Office.

SECTION 2. The judicial Power shall extend to all Cases, in Law and Equity, arising under this Constitution, the Laws of the United States, and Treaties made, or which shall be made, under their Authority;—to all Cases affecting Ambassadors, other public Ministers and Consuls;—to all Cases of admiralty and maritime Jurisdiction;—to Controversies to which the United States shall be a Party;—to Controversies between two or more States;—between a State and Citizens of another State;—between Citizens of different States;—between Citizens of the same State claiming Lands under Grants of different States, and between a State, or the Citizens thereof, and foreign States, Citizens or Subjects.

In all Cases affecting Ambassadors, other public Ministers and Consuls, and those in which a State shall be Party, the supreme Court shall have original Jurisdiction. In all the other Cases before mentioned, the supreme Court shall have appellate Jurisdiction, both as to Law and Fact, with such Exceptions, and under such Regulations as the Congress shall make.

The trial of all Crimes, except in Cases of Impeachment, shall be by Jury; and such Trial shall be held in the State where the said Crimes shall have been committed; but when not committed within any State, the Trial shall be at such Place or Places as the Congress may by Law have directed.

SECTION 3. Treason against the United States, shall consist only in levying War against them, or in adhering to their Enemies, giving them Aid and Comfort. No Person shall be convicted of Treason unless on the Testimony of two Witnesses to the same overt Act, or on Confession in open Court.

The Congress shall have power to declare the Punishment of Treason, but no Attainder of Treason shall work Corruption of Blood, or Forfeiture except during the Life of the Person attainted.

ARTICLE IV

SECTION 1. Full Faith and Credit shall be given in each State to the public Acts, Records, and judicial Proceedings of every other State. And the Congress may by general Laws prescribe the Manner in which such Acts, Records and Proceedings shall be proved, and the Effect thereof.

SECTION 2. The Citizens of each State shall be entitled to all Privileges and Immunities of Citizens in the several States.

A Person charged in any State with Treason, Felony, or other Crime, who shall flee from Justice, and be found in another State, shall on demand of the executive Authority of the State from which he fled, be delivered up, to be removed to the State having Jurisdiction of the Crime.

No Person held to Service or Labour in one State, under the Laws thereof, escaping into another, shall, in Consequence of any Law or Regulation therein, be discharged from such Service or Labour, but shall be delivered up on Claim of the Party to whom such Service or Labour may be due.

SECTION 3. New States may be admitted by the Congress into this Union; but no new State shall be formed or erected within the Jurisdiction of any other State; nor any State be formed by the Junction of two or more States, or parts of States, without the Consent of the Legislatures of the States concerned as well as of the Congress.

The Congress shall have Power to dispose of and make all needful Rules and Regulations respecting the Territory or other Property belonging to the United States; and nothing in this Constitution shall be so construed as to Prejudice any Claims of the United States, or of any particular State.

SECTION 4. The United States shall guarantee to every State in this Union a Republican Form of Government, and shall protect each of them against Invasion; and on Application of the Legislature, or of the Executive (when the Legislature cannot be convened) against domestic Violence.

ARTICLE V

The Congress, whenever two thirds of both Houses shall deem it necessary, shall propose Amendments to this Constitution, or, on the Application of the Legislatures of two thirds of the several States, shall call a Convention for proposing Amendments, which, in either Case, shall be valid to all Intents and Purposes, as part of this Constitution, when ratified by the Legislatures of three fourths of the several States, or by Conventions in three fourths thereof, as the one or the other Mode of Ratification may be proposed by the Congress; Provided that no Amendment which may be made prior to the Year One thousand eight hundred and eight shall in any Manner affect the first and fourth Clauses in the Ninth Section of the first Article; and that no State, without its Consent, shall be deprived of its equal Suffrage in the Senate.

ARTICLE VI

All Debts contracted and Engagements entered into, before the Adoption of this Constitution, shall be as valid against the United States under this Constitution, as under the Confederation.

This Constitution, and the Laws of the United States which shall be made in Pursuance thereof; and all Treaties made, or which shall be made, under the Authority of the United States, shall be the supreme Law of the Land; and the Judges in every State shall be bound thereby, any Thing in the Constitution or Laws of any State to the Contrary notwithstanding.

The Senators and Representatives before mentioned, and the Members of the several State Legislatures, and all executive and judicial Officers, both of the United States and of the several States, shall be bound by Oath or

Affirmation, to support this Constitution; but no religious Test shall ever be required as a Qualification to any Office or public Trust under the United States.

ARTICLE VII

The Ratification of the Conventions of nine States shall be sufficient for the Establishment of this Constitution between the States so ratifying the Same.

Done in Convention by the Unanimous Consent of the States present the Seventeenth Day of September in the Year of our Lord one thousand seven hundred and Eighty seven and of the Independence of the United States of America the Twelfth. In Witness whereof We have hereunto subscribed our Names. [Signatures omitted.]

ARTICLES IN ADDITION TO, AND AMENDMENT OF, THE CONSTITUTION OF THE UNITED STATES OF AMERICA, PROPOSED BY CONGRESS, AND RATIFIED BY THE LEGISLATURES OF THE SEVERAL STATES, PURSUANT TO THE FIFTH ARTICLE OF THE ORIGINAL CONSTITUTION.

AMENDMENT I

Congress shall make no law respecting an establishment of religion, or prohibiting the free exercise thereof; or abridging the freedom of speech, or of the press; or the right of the people peaceably to assemble, and to petition the Government for a redress of grievances.

AMENDMENT II

A well regulated Militia, being necessary to the security of a free State, the right of the people to keep and bear Arms, shall not be infringed.

AMENDMENT III

No Soldier shall, in time of peace be quartered in any house, without the consent of the Owner, nor in time of war, but in a manner to be prescribed by law.

AMENDMENT IV

The right of the people to be secure in their persons, houses, papers, and effects, against unreasonable searches and seizures, shall not be violated, and no Warrants shall issue, but upon probable cause, supported by Oath or affirmation, and particularly describing the place to be searched, and the persons or things to be seized.

AMENDMENT V

No person shall be held to answer for a capital, or otherwise infamous crime, unless on a presentment or indictment of a Grand Jury, except in cases arising in the land or naval forces, or in the Militia, when in actual service in time of War or public danger; nor shall any person be subject for the same offence to be twice put in jeopardy of life or limb; nor shall be compelled in any criminal case to be a witness against himself, nor be deprived of life, liberty, or property, without due process of law; nor shall private property be taken for public use, without just compensation.

AMENDMENT VI

In all criminal prosecutions, the accused shall enjoy the right to a speedy and public trial, by an impartial jury of the State and district wherein the crime shall have been committed, which district shall have been previously ascertained by law, and to be informed of the nature and cause of the accusation; to be confronted with the witnesses against him; to have compulsory process for obtaining witnesses in his favor, and to have the Assistance of Counsel for his defence.

AMENDMENT VII

In suits at common law, where the value in controversy shall exceed twenty dollars, the right of trial by jury shall be preserved, and no fact tried by a jury, shall be otherwise re-examined in any Court of the United States, than according to the rules of the common law.

AMENDMENT VIII

Excessive bail shall not be required, nor excessive fines imposed, nor cruel and unusual punishments inflicted.

AMENDMENT IX

The enumeration in the Constitution, of certain rights, shall not be construed to deny or disparage others retained by the people.

AMENDMENT X

The powers not delegated to the United States by the Constitution, nor prohibited by it to the States, are reserved to the States respectively, or to the people.

AMENDMENT XI [1798]

The Judicial power of the United States shall not be construed to extend to any suit in law or equity, commenced or prosecuted against one of the United States by Citizens of another State, or by Citizens or Subjects of any Foreign State.

AMENDMENT XII [1804]

The Electors shall meet in their respective states and vote by ballot for President and Vice President, one of whom, at least, shall not be an inhabitant of the same state with themselves; they shall name in their ballots the person voted for as President, and in distinct ballots the person voted for as Vice President, and they shall make distinct lists of all persons voted for as President, and of all persons voted for as Vice President, and of the number of votes for each, which lists they shall sign and certify, and transmit sealed to the seat of the government of the United States, directed to the President of the Senate;—The President of the Senate shall, in presence of the Senate and House of Representatives, open all the certificates and the votes shall then be counted;—The person having the greatest number of votes for President, shall be the President, if such number be a majority of the whole number of Electors appointed; and if no person have such majority, then from the persons having the highest numbers not exceeding three on the list of those voted for as President, the House of Representatives shall choose immediately, by ballot, the President. But in choosing the President, the votes shall be taken by states, the representation from each state having one vote; a quorum for this purpose shall consist of a member or members from two-thirds of the states, and a majority of all the states shall be necessary to a choice. And if the House of Representatives shall not choose a President whenever the right of choice shall devolve upon them, before the fourth day of March next following, then the Vice President shall act as President, as in the case of the death or other constitutional disability of the President.—The person having the greatest number of votes as Vice President, shall be the Vice President, if such number be a majority of the whole number of Electors appointed, and if no person have a majority, then from the two highest numbers on the list, the Senate shall choose the Vice President; a quorum for the purpose shall consist of two-thirds of the whole number of Senators, and a majority of the whole number shall be necessary to a choice. But no person constitutionally ineligible to the office of President shall be eligible to that of Vice President of the United States.

AMENDMENT XIII [1865]

SECTION 1. Neither slavery nor involuntary servitude, except as a punishment for crime whereof the party shall have been duly convicted, shall exist within the United States, or any place subject to their jurisdiction.

SECTION 2. Congress shall have power to enforce this article by appropriate legislation.

AMENDMENT XIV [1868]

SECTION 1. All persons born or naturalized in the United States, and subject to the jurisdiction thereof, are citizens of the United States and of the State wherein they reside. No State shall make or enforce any law which shall abridge the privileges or immunities of citizens of the United States; nor shall any State deprive any person of life, liberty, or property, without due process of law; nor deny to any person within its jurisdiction the equal protection of the laws.

SECTION 2. Representatives shall be apportioned among the several States according to their respective numbers, counting the whole number of persons in each State, excluding Indians not taxed. But when the right to vote at any election for the choice of electors for President and Vice President of the United States, Representatives in Congress, the Executive and Judicial officers of a State, or the members of the Legislature thereof, is denied to any of the male inhabitants of such State, being twenty-one years of age, and citizens of the United States, or in any way abridged, except for participation in rebellion, or other crime, the basis of representation therein shall be reduced in the proportion which the number of such male citizens shall bear to the whole number of male citizens twenty-one years of age in such State.

SECTION 3. No person shall be a Senator or Representative in Congress, or elector of President and Vice President, or hold any office, civil or military, under the United States, or under any State, who, having previously taken an oath, as a member of Congress, or as an officer of the United States, or as a member of any State legislature, or as an executive or judicial officer of any State, to support the Constitution of the United States, shall have engaged in insurrection or rebellion against the same, or given aid or comfort to the enemies thereof. But Congress may by a vote of two-thirds of each House, remove such disability.

SECTION 4. The validity of the public debt of the United States, authorized by law, including debts incurred for payment of pensions and bounties for services in suppressing insurrection or rebellion shall not be questioned. But neither the United States nor any State shall assume or pay any debt or obligation incurred in aid of insurrection or rebellion against the United States, or any claim for the loss or emancipation of any slaves; but all such debts, obligations and claims shall be held illegal and void.

SECTION 5. The Congress shall have power to enforce, by appropriate legislation, the provisions of this article.

AMENDMENT XV [1870]

SECTION 1. The right of citizens of the United States to vote shall not be denied or abridged by the United States or by any State on account of race, color, or previous condition of servitude.

SECTION 2. The Congress shall have power to enforce this article by appropriate legislation.

AMENDMENT XVI [1913]

The Congress shall have power to lay and collect taxes on incomes, from whatever source derived, without apportionment among the several States, and without regard to any census or enumeration.

AMENDMENT XVII [1913]

The Senate of the United States shall be composed of two Senators from each State, elected by the people thereof, for six years; and each Senator shall have one vote. The electors in each State shall have the qualifications requisite for electors of the most numerous branch of the State legislatures.

When vacancies happen in the representation of any State in the Senate, the executive authority of such State shall issue writs of election to fill such vacancies: *Provided,* That the legislature of any State may empower the executive thereof to make temporary appointments until the people fill the vacancies by election as the legislature may direct.

This amendment shall not be so construed as to affect the election or term of any Senator chosen before it becomes valid as part of the Constitution.

AMENDMENT XVIII [1919]

SECTION 1. After one year from the ratification of this article the manufacture, sale, or transportation of intoxicating liquors within, the importation thereof into, or the exportation thereof from the United States and all territory subject to the jurisdiction thereof for beverage purposes is hereby prohibited.

SECTION 2. The Congress and the several States shall have concurrent power to enforce this article by appropriate legislation.

SECTION 3. This article shall be inoperative unless it shall have been ratified as an amendment to the Constitution by the legislatures of the several States, as provided in the Constitution, within seven years from the date of the submission hereof to the States by the Congress.

AMENDMENT XIX [1920]

The right of citizens of the United States to vote shall not be denied or abridged by the United States or by any State on account of sex.

Congress shall have power to enforce this article by appropriate legislation.

AMENDMENT XX [1933]

SECTION 1. The terms of the President and Vice President shall end at noon on the 20th day of January, and the terms of Senators and Representatives at noon on the 3d day of January, of the years in which such terms would have ended if this article had not been ratified; and the terms of their successors shall then begin.

SECTION 2. The Congress shall assemble at least once in every year, and such meeting shall begin at noon on the 3d day of January, unless they shall by law appoint a different day.

SECTION 3. If, at the time fixed for the beginning of the term of the President, the President elect shall have died, the Vice President elect shall become President. If a President shall not have been chosen before the time fixed for the beginning of his term, or if the President elect shall have failed to qualify, then the Vice President elect shall act as President until a President shall have qualified; and the Congress may by law provide for the case wherein neither a President elect nor a Vice President elect shall have qualified, declaring who shall then act as President, or the manner in which one who is to act shall be selected, and such person shall act accordingly until a President or Vice President shall have qualified.

SECTION 4. The Congress may by law provide for the case of the death of any of the persons from whom the House of Representatives may choose a President whenever the right of choice shall have devolved upon them, and for the case of the death of any of the persons from whom the Senate may choose a Vice President whenever the right of choice shall have devolved upon them.

SECTION 5. Sections 1 and 2 shall take effect on the 15th day of October following the ratification of this article.

SECTION 6. This article shall be inoperative unless it shall have been ratified as an amendment to the Constitution by the legislatures of three-fourths of the several States within seven years from the date of its submission.

AMENDMENT XXI [1933]

SECTION 1. The eighteenth article of amendment to the Constitution of the United States is hereby repealed.

SECTION 2. The transportation or importation into any State, Territory, or Possession of the United States for delivery or use therein of intoxicating liquors, in violation of the laws thereof, is hereby prohibited.

SECTION 3. This article shall be inoperative unless it shall have been ratified as an amendment to the Constitution by conventions in the several States, as provided in the Constitution, within seven years from the date of the submission hereof to the States by the Congress.

AMENDMENT XXII [1951]

SECTION 1. No person shall be elected to the office of the President more than twice, and no person who has held the office of President, or acted as President, for more than two years of a term to which some other person was elected President shall be elected to the office of the President more than once. But this Article shall not apply to any person holding the office of President when this Article was proposed by the Congress, and shall not prevent any person who may be holding the office of President, or acting as President, during the term within which this Article becomes operative from holding the office of President or acting as President during the remainder of such term.

SECTION 2. This article shall be inoperative unless it shall have been ratified as an amendment to the Constitution by the legislatures of three-fourths of the several States within seven years from the date of its submission to the States by the Congress.

AMENDMENT XXIII [1961]

Section 1. The District constituting the seat of Government of the United States shall appoint in such manner as Congress may direct:

A number of electors of President and Vice President equal to the whole number of Senators and Representatives in Congress to which the District would be entitled if it were a State, but in no event more than the least populous State; they shall be in addition to those appointed by the States, but they shall be considered, for the purposes of the election of President and Vice President, to be electors appointed by a State; and they shall meet in the District and perform such duties as provided by the twelfth article of amendment.

Section 2. The Congress shall have power to enforce this article by appropriate legislation.

AMENDMENT XXIV [1964]

Section 1. The right of citizens of the United States to vote in any primary or other election for President or Vice President, for electors for President or Vice President, or for Senator or Representative in Congress, shall not be denied or abridged by the United States or any State by reason of failure to pay any poll tax or other tax.

Section 2. The Congress shall have power to enforce this article by appropriate legislation.

AMENDMENT XXV [1967]

Section 1. In case of the removal of the President from office or of his death or resignation, the Vice President shall become President.

Section 2. Whenever there is a vacancy in the office of the Vice President, the President shall nominate a Vice President who shall take office upon confirmation by a majority vote of both Houses of Congress.

Section 3. Whenever the President transmits to the President pro tempore of the Senate and the Speaker of the House of Representatives his written declaration that he is unable to discharge the powers and duties of his office, and until he transmits to them a written declaration to the contrary, such powers and duties shall be discharged by the Vice President as Acting President.

Section 4. Whenever the Vice President and a majority of either the principal officers of the executive departments or of such other body as Congress may by law provide, transmit to the President pro tempore of the Senate and the Speaker of the House of Representatives their written declaration that the President is unable to discharge the powers and duties of his office, the Vice President shall immediately assume the powers and duties of the office as Acting President.

Thereafter, when the President transmits to the President pro tempore of the Senate and the Speaker of the House of Representatives his written declaration that no inability exists, he shall resume the powers and duties of his office unless the Vice President and a majority of either the principal officers of the executive department or of such other body as Congress may by law provide, transmit within four days to the President pro tempore of the Senate and the Speaker of the House of Representatives their written declaration that the President is unable to discharge the powers and duties of his office. Thereupon Congress shall decide the issue, assembling within forty-eight hours for that purpose if not in session. If the Congress, within twenty-one days after receipt of the latter written declaration, or, if Congress is not in session, within twenty-one days after Congress is required to assemble, determines by two-thirds vote of both Houses that the President is unable to discharge the powers and duties of his office, the Vice President shall continue to discharge the same as Acting President; otherwise, the President shall resume the powers and duties of his office.

AMENDMENT XXVI [1971]

SECTION 1. The right of citizens of the United States, who are eighteen years of age or older, to vote shall not be denied or abridged by the United States or by any State on account of age.

SECTION 2. The Congress shall have power to enforce this article by appropriate legislation.

AMENDMENT XXVII (PROPOSED)

SECTION 1. Equality of rights under the law shall not be denied or abridged by the United States or by any state on account of sex.

SECTION 2. The Congress shall have the power to enforce, by appropriate legislation, the provisions of this article.

SECTION 3. This amendment shall take effect two years after the date of ratification.

DATE DUE